WHAT'S THE PLAN?

Is It God's Plan?

WHAT'S THE PLAN?

Is It God's Plan?

BY ROBERT J. SULLIVAN, PHD

EQUIP PRESS

Colorado Springs

What Is Your Plan? Is it God's Plan?
Copyright © 2022 Robert J. Sullivan, PhD

All rights reserved. No part of this publication may be reproduced, distributed, or transmitted in any form or by any means, without prior written permission.

Scripture quotations marked (ESV) are taken from The ESV® Bible (The Holy Bible, English Standard Version®) copyright © 2001 by Crossway, a publishing minis-try of Good News Publishers. ESV® Text Edition: 2011. The ESV® text has been reproduced in cooperation with and by permission of Good News Publishers.
Unauthorized reproduction of this publication is prohibited. Used by permission.
All rights reserved.

Scripture quotations marked (KJV) are taken from the King James Bible. Accessed on Bible Gateway at www.BibleGateway.com.

Scripture quotations marked (NASB) are taken from the New American Standard Bible® (NASB), copyright © 1960, 1962, 1963, 1968, 1971, 1972, 1973, 1975, 1977, 1995 by The Lockman Foundation, www.Lockman.org. Used by permission.

Scripture quotations marked (NIV) are taken from the Holy Bible, New International Version. Copyright © 1973, 1978, 1984, 2011 by Biblica, Inc.® Used by permission. All rights reserved worldwide.

Scripture quotations marked (NKJV) are taken from the New King James Version®. Copyright © 1982 by Thomas Nelson, Inc. Used by permission. All rights reserved.

Scripture quotations marked (NLT) are taken from the Holy Bible, New Living Translation, copyright © 1996, 2004, 2015 by Tyndale House Foundation. Used by permission of Tyndale House Publishers, Inc., Carol Stream, Illinois 60188. All rights reserved.

Scripture quotations marked (NRSV) are taken from the New Revised Standard Version Bible, copyright © 1989 the Division of Christian Education of the National

Scripture quotations taken from the Amplified® Bible (AMP), Copyright © 2015 by The Lockman Foundation Used by permission. www.Lockman.org

First Edition: 2022
What Is Your Plan? / Robert J. Sullivan
Title of Book / Author Name
Paperback ISBN: 978-1-951304-96-6
eBook ISBN: 978-1-951304-97-3

DEDICATION
To Lea, Alec, Cole, and Caesar.
You are my true earthly and eternal calling.

TABLE OF CONTENTS

1. Close the Gap 1
2. Why or Why Not? 13
3. The Road Traveled By GPS 27
4. Everyone Has a Plan 35
5. Shame and Its Residue 45
6. The Comparison Trap 61
7. The Comfort Zone 75
8. Instant Gratification 87
9. Consequences—What Can Go Wrong? 97
10. Decisions, Decisions, Decisions 107
11. The Middle 115
12. The Original Title of this Book and Its Meaning 125

CHAPTER 1
CLOSE THE GAP

What if we start our journey with a story? I work at a university. Like many universities, we host "preview weekends," where both parents and prospective students get a daylong look under the hood. I emcee *Meet the Professors* sessions as part of my responsibilities. High school students, parents, and faculty crowd into an often-overflowing classroom to get to know one another. My spiel stresses student-faculty connection, so everyone introduces themselves with some fun icebreakers. I conclude by splitting everyone into major groups, but never before noting God's calling in their lives and emphasizing our role in helping them discover the divine design for their life.

Normally, these sessions devolve into small talk before everyone moves on to the next event. However, a few years ago, a *Meet the Professors* session failed to follow the blueprint. A father used the transition window to ask me a cutting question: "Why do you talk about God so much? People are talking to me all day about faith but not education. What gives?"

He pointed out that he had devoted twenty years to the mission field, so his question was not coming from a secular humanist. Rather, he said, he was a concerned father seeking confirmation that tuition dollars would deliver a solid return on his investment.

My response? Well, I recall getting a little defensive, which allowed me to revert to my first language: sarcasm. "Yes, why would *we,* who represent a Christian university, talk about God so much?" My head spun with questions: Is he challenging our sincerity; does he think we are hiding something?

Bottom line, the man merely wanted assurance that his son would obtain a college education, graduate, get a job, and move out on his own. It is a fair expectation given the prevailing higher-education price tag. I refer to this as the commodification of higher education. This mindset identifies college as a tool for obtaining a fiscal accrual-driven credential, which is an accurate vision for college education. College serves as the bridge connecting childhood to maturity, and it is understandable that those toting the note would expect the service we offer to result in a gainfully employed, bill-paying adult.

The father's vision was accurate—just not complete. His questions spurred hand wringing and large-scale reflection and, eventually, the book you are reading.

As professors at a Christian university, we are in the mind-molding business, ala Romans 12:2. I want to be a top-shelf molder of minds, both young and old. But treating higher education as a product reduces the potential benefits to a list of marketable skills. Skills are critical, to be sure, but believers must also identify why God blessed them with a particular set of skills.

Treating Christian higher education as a commodity has a second drawback: it models the dualistic Christian life. You know the one where our Sunday-morning self remains separate from our Monday-through-Saturday self? The one that disconnects work from faith, and life from faith? The one most Christians pursue.

This is where the chili meets the cheese. Is a college degree a credential that primarily ensures employability and security, or is it a calling card for the expansion and greater impact of God's Kingdom?

I have spent a considerable portion of my career mentoring college students. College means fun! It also means angst. What does the future look like? What are God's plans for me? What is my calling? How do you or I know God's calling for our lives? When we examine how we spend our lives, how do we know we are following God's calling? Tough questions.

This book does not answer these questions completely. (Sorry if you bought the book looking for such answers.) My theological training consists of six hours of Bible courses and a lifetime of Sunday school. However, you do not need an Augustinian level of scriptural knowledge to understand that every calling not only honors God (even lawyers and politicians) but also directly contributes to eternity.

My writing approach involves connecting with readers on a personal level. God bestows gifts and talents upon each of us to equip us to have an eternal impact. My goal is not to find definitive answers to these eternal questions but to help readers develop an eternal vision that merges calling and career, whether the daily commute ends at a construction firm, a diner, church, seminary, law firm, financial office, or home. And more crucially, stick to that eternal vision regardless of circumstances.

But how do you know your path is God's will? *And to what extent?*

My wife and I support a friend named Elly financially. Armed with an ASL teaching certification, God called Elly, or Elly believes God called her, to serve the deaf community. In fact, Elly's path led her to Honduras—and not just Honduras, but a rural Honduras community. She works with several deaf children who previously failed absent a support system. No support for a deaf individual often means no communication, and many of Elly's students could not talk to their families or anyone else prior to Elly's arrival.

How did Elly end up serving deaf children in rural Honduras? After college, she started teaching in a public school near her hometown. Two years later, she received a call from a wealthy Honduran family in need of a tutor for their deaf daughter. Elly felt God called her to make the move, so she resigned from a stable teaching job and moved to Honduras. The opportunity proved to be everything she had hoped for and more, but the family decided the child no longer needed tutoring once she reached a certain age. So that left dear Elly in limbo, which meant the Honduran experiment was ending. However, five families with deaf children in the small, tight-knit community reached out to her for similar help. Again, God's providential bounty overflowed with riches!

But this bounty carried complications, with the chief challenge being financial. These families were penniless, with barely enough resources for food and shelter. Elly herself needed food and shelter, but this "opportunity" did not include compensation. She instinctively reached out to friends and family members to gauge the possibility of support. And while the economic realities Elly faced were daunting, the cost-of-living needs offered hope. Elly determined the subsistence level was less than $1,000 monthly, but she targeted that clean, round number so she might afford needed educational supplies. The Lord provided.

Elly's Honduran season is reaching five years as you read this, with a bright future very much in play. She even started a nonprofit, which has seen fundraising numbers escalate. Of course, Elly very much realizes God could move her and continually prays that her heart and mind are only open to serving Him.

HOW DO YOU KNOW?

Does your story mirror Elly's adventures? Or is your walk tame by comparison? Is that bad? Does God expect us to take more risks? After all, faith means jumping without a net, right?

What would God have you do?

The socioeconomic/work environment during the historical era of the Bible narrative fascinates me as a social scientist. Developing a better understanding of the ancient daily grind provides context for understanding the gospel narrative. The movement transcended class and wealth status, as servants could evangelize their wealthy employers or masters and vice versa. Additionally, the movement leveraged business networks and ports to spread the message.[1]

The Gospels describe how Jesus recruited the disciples while also explaining their sacrifices. Luke's account of Jesus recruiting Simon Peter, James, and John while they were fishing is a wonderful example. It is especially interesting to read the Gospels and determine how Jesus chose and recruited the disciples. These books also describe what the disciples left behind. What did the twelve sacrifice to follow Jesus?

> One day as Jesus was standing by the Lake of Gennesaret, the people were crowding around him and listening to the word of God. He saw at the water's edge two boats, left there by the fishermen, who were washing their nets. He got into one of the boats, the one belonging to Simon, and asked him to put out a little from shore. Then he sat down and taught the people from the boat.
> When he had finished speaking, he said to Simon, "Put out into deep water, and let down the nets for a catch."

---

[1] Stark, Rodney

> Simon answered, "Master, we've worked hard all night and haven't caught anything. But because you say so, I will let down the nets." When they had done so, they caught such a large number of fish that their nets began to break. So they signaled their partners in the other boat to come and help them, and they came and filled both boats so full that they began to sink.
> When Simon Peter saw this, he fell at Jesus' knees and said, "Go away from me, Lord; I am a sinful man!" For he and all his companions were astonished at the catch of fish they had taken, and so were James and John, the sons of Zebedee, Simon's partners.
> Then Jesus said to Simon, "Don't be afraid; from now on you will fish for people." So they pulled their boats up on shore, left everything and followed him (Luke 5:1-13, English Standard Version).[2]

This passage threads the needle. Jesus is directly calling the future disciples to step out on faith. Christians often struggle with interpreting God's calling for their lives, but this is clear.

Most Christians struggle in identifying with scriptural figures such as the disciples. Do you remember hearing the stories in Sunday school during your formative years? Personally, it's hard for me to envision characters from Sunday school coloring workbooks or puzzles as real people with real problems. However, Simon Peter, James, and John were real people with real responsibilities.[3] Shows like *The Chosen* give us an idea of how real these guys were. The Savior approached them during their efforts to satisfy family needs, their financial burdens, and their business interests. This is a real-life example of what we are

---

[2] Luke 5:1-13 English Standard Version)
[3] We might call this a workplace conversion!

talking about in this book.

Luke is hardly the only gospel author detailing that Jesus called the fishermen to follow Him, but only his account includes the fishing story.[4] It also consists of two commands from Jesus. They are similar yet distinct in critical ways, including the outcomes they yield. I want to examine these distinctions and discuss what they say regarding career and calling.

Command #1: Jesus instructs the anglers to let down their nets in verse 4.

Indeed, drop your nets and good things will happen. This command/suggestion carries weight because their workday was over, with little to show for it. This reminds me of the time I went fly-fishing. I spent loads of money renting equipment and got sopping wet only to strike out.[5] However, they fished to put food on the table. The stakes were infinitely higher.

So how might we possibly interpret this command? Here are a few options.

1. Letting God run things is a good idea. It yields success! We might refer to this as the American interpretation. God is good for business, so to speak. I do not mean to sound that harsh, but some people think that way. Church is a networking opportunity. My favorite is people who claim to seek God's will, but His "will" always seems to help them or align with their goals. Of course, "giving it all to God" will maximize our blessings. That said, those blessings might not be the ones we wanted.

2. Letting God run things is a good idea, but the process could be uncomfortable. We really have no idea the road we will travel. The path will get rocky, but He has our back. The difficult times are part of the plan and only increase our faith. Therefore, we as believers should count our blessings and move forward without fear, even in the face of fear. Rely on God's roadmap/GPS and never deviate from it.

---

[4] Luke, Mark, Matthew, Working Preacher
[5] Which was incredibly frustrating because we could see the fish! They ignored us!

3. Letting God run things is a good idea, but we must understand outcomes could be different. We give our careers over to God and accept the outcome. We discuss our career criteria in chapter 3 by comparing our worldly criteria with God's criteria. What do we deem important in selecting a path versus what God deems important? This analysis distinguishes the temporary from the eternal.

Okay, those interpretations challenge us. We may never experience our deepest desires, hopes, or dreams. World domination goes elsewhere. Still, our efforts with God's help can yield results demanding world respect and perhaps envy while also honoring God's eternal Kingdom.

Command #2: Jesus Commands them to lay down their worldly possessions and follow Him in Verse 10.

In addition, they readily comply without hesitation, at least according to Scripture. Laying down everything? This is a different deal entirely.

What do they "lay down" specifically?
1. They gave up their bounty.
2. They left the huge haul on the shore! Who does that? This also means something bigger as the future disciples reject food and sustenance.
3. They ignored perhaps the most successful day of their careers!
4. Catching boatloads of fish surely accorded recognition and accolades among peers, yet they left it all on the shores of the Lake of Gennesaret. They sacrificed both sustenance and success! Honestly, would you ask Jesus to return tomorrow and bring his fish finder?
5. They gave up their means of support and livelihood.
6. Lifelong careers gone like vapors in the wind. Yes, the disciples surrendered their personal sense of self-worth as they left behind their sense of identity. Yet they also left their sense of security behind.
7. They left their resources.
8. The nets represented an investment in their careers and lives. Peter, James, and John toiled and sweated merely to

purchase the tools of their trade.[6] Consider your investment of time, talent, and treasure in your career. They rejected it all for a Kingdom calling. Every piece of personal and professional capital set aside for a higher calling. The first command carried several possible interpretations, but this command is clear, and the disciples respond to it accordingly. They surrendered/sacrificed everything for Jesus. Why did they do this? Your reading will reveal that later, but I have another probing question to ask before we get to that point.

Could you do that? Leave every sense of comfort, security, and sense of self-worth in the dust and start anew? As a bonus, you not only have zero ideas of the outcome or even what you would be doing on a daily basis and how you would be doing it. Did God wire you that way, or do you toil in the comfort zone?

I am not ripping your choices either way! My path has included the road more traveled several times. It hardly makes us less Christian to justify avoiding the boiling cauldron of pressure that the unknown brings to the table. Most folks do the same thing. The only problem is this is not what God wants or needs from us.

God wants us to flip our thinking when it comes to comfort and fear—the connective tissue running through the Bible. It is human nature to seek comfort or security. Humans pursue comfort in most every aspect of life. Think about why you chose your career, church membership, community, politics, relationships, group "memberships," and other social subsets. But while we seek comfort, God plans to pursue that which we fear.

More importantly (perhaps): Are you called to do that? Does God expect followers to drop and reject everything? On the other hand, do you identify with one of the first command interpretations? We can all agree there is clearly a large distinction between the two commands, which encompasses process, sacrifice, and outcome. I coin this the Gennesaret Gap to honor Luke's "conversion version," even though it may not be the catchiest option!

---

[6] Or did folks normally make their own nets?

THE GENNESARET GAP

I chose the title because this project essentially serves as a gap analysis. What is a gap analysis? While this is the purpose of chapter 2, a gap analysis is an evaluation to determine the distance between where you are and where you want or need to be based on chosen criteria. Moreover, the criteria is critical, as chapter 2 explains. The analysis concludes when evaluators determine how much it will cost to achieve the goal. Therefore, our journey will include identifying the criteria, examining or analyzing them, and calculating the gap-closing cost/benefit ratio by determining the steps and sacrifices God requires for each of us.

This book explores the gap between how believers view God's calling and its true nature—the chasm between our worldly hopes and what it truly means to surrender to God's calling. Specifically, this journey should explain why and how to close that gap. We also determine what closing the gap means. What sacrifices are required?

We spend this time addressing several gap-related questions. First, why does the gap exist? Well, our human (sin) nature identifies the criteria that indicates a successful, happy existence. Chapter 2 contrasts these criteria with God's eternal criteria. These benchmarks of the good life flow from various sources. The human condition (especially Americans) naturally defaults to self-preservation. Chapter 3 maps out our journey through the book. Chapters 4–8 compare each earthly criterion to its matching eternal criterion as we determine the gap-closing cost. Chapter 4 explores how this drives our plan and why our own blueprint supersedes God's design. Chapter 5 explains how circumstances perhaps move us to deviate from the godly design as well as how the residue of shame short-circuits our calling. Again, this is less about the power of life's challenges but more about how we respond. Additionally, life is about competition, but the accompanying comparison trap hamstrings our eternal capacity. Chapter 6 describes how our life with others weakens our appreciation of God's blessings in our own life.

Chapter 7 examines our pursuit of comfort and God's calling so that we flip our thinking regarding embracing fear and rejecting the pursuit of security and popularity by giving it all over to God. Additionally, the modern human brain is wired to instant stimulus response, but chapter 8 extols the virtues of waiting patiently for compounding blessings. Chapter 9 both finishes and synthesizes the criteria section by contrasting the motivations of Kingdom builders and empire seekers.

While these chapters paint a bleak picture of our calling condition, they also prescribe gap-closing treatments while introducing readers to special "gap fillers" or believers who effectively closed the gap. We will meet folks such as Elly, who sacrificed everything and dropped their nets for an eternal purpose. Yet we will also meet J, who never left his job for an exotic, untapped mission field but still managed to sacrifice every working day and its bounty for the Kingdom. Chapter 10 exclaims the importance of making wise decisions but also choosing the proper source of said decisions. Chapter 11 explains how this world and our purpose in it do not always make sense and why that is a beautiful part of God's eternal design. Chapter 12 concludes our time together by explaining the original topics for this book.

My apologies if this all sounds formal, official, or corporate. Please allow me to share a few caveats to ease your mind.

1. This all sounds so "sciencey," but really, this book is about relationships.
2. Yes, chapter 2 establishes a narrative format or structure best described as the scientific method. However, each chapter dives deeper into your relationship with Jesus. The plan involves unpacking your calling.
3. This is not a textbook!
4. Yes, I teach college, but this is not a textbook. My goal was to pen a joy generator, helping you ponder your calling and motivations for said calling as opposed to developing a narrow curriculum. I added a few tables and graphics but tried to keep those to a minimum. You will find no homework or assignments in this book. Granted, the website includes a downloadable workbook, but it is completely optional. I promise!
5. Stories drive the narrative.
6. Biblical stories, yes, of course, but also contemporary yarns about believers like you and me grappling over how God plans to use them. There might even be a few stories

involving your humble host/author. My hope is to hear your stories someday!
7. This book is not judging you or anyone else.
8. This work is formed from my own thoughts and struggles with worldly affirmation. The criteria chapters chronicle my challenges, although the assumption is that they are universal. Who doesn't yearn for more money or fame? The clarion call beckons me like everyone. My demons live in this book.
9. This book is not telling you to drop everything.
10. Luke 5 ends with the disciples dropping everything to follow Jesus. Am I asking you to follow suit? Frankly, my focus is your mindset and motives as opposed to outcomes. However, we can all agree that should be our attitude. My thesis certainly poses that we should all possess the willingness to abandon our earthly comforts.
11. This project is structured to develop the conversation, not serve as the entire conversation.
12. The companion website provides free exercises to crystallize your vision of God's design for your calling. Please check it out either while reading or once you are finished reading the entire book. The activities align with specific chapters, so doing your "homework" after finishing a chapter is optimal, as it injects additional critical thinking of the concepts while setting the table for the next chapter. Also, the activities provide an awesome tool for Sunday school classes or Bible study groups working through Gennesaret Gap.

And we will use St. Peter and his life to guide us. What better teacher than Peter (and other friends) to guide us to sacrificial calling? Peter the rock, who left a humble fisherman's life to follow Jesus without fully understanding the path that lay before him. The leading disciple whose arrogance and temper often overshadowed his contributions to the movement and created shame he had to work through. The early church stalwart engaging in a war of words with the Pharisees and other religious leaders. The missionary who came to (verbal) blows with Paul over the plight of Gentile converts.

That said, Peter was also steadfast in the face of adversity. He continued onward even in the face of death. Peter did not blink when Jesus explained in grisly detail how the apostle would die—the uneducated fisherman who penned some of the most beautiful and lasting Scripture. Peter's life is our prism, including every success, failure, and sacrifice.

My fervent hope in writing this book is to develop a community of believers engaging in everyday economic evangelism where God has planted them, whether for the balance of their careers or for a season. Please take a moment to peruse the other resources, blog posts, and podcasts as we work through our callings together. Please know that I want to hear from you and whether this experience has proven transformative on any level.

Moreover, what are those results? What are my hopes and dreams for you upon completing this book? What do I want you to do? Well, aligning our hopes and dreams with God's eternal plan and priorities would be a great start. Therefore, our journey proceeds by comparing what believers want to achieve during their careers with the outcomes God wants.

CHAPTER 2
WHY OR WHY NOT?

God blessed me with numerous friends studying in religion and philosophy majors during my undergrad years. They constantly warned me about one professor. He was *the* philosophy and ethics professor for our little slice of higher education. My senior year included his ethics course. This instructor was somewhat notorious for using a hard curve in his courses, thus leaving most students with a C. Some liked this. Many did not. This student fell into the latter camp.

Yet most every student loved his classes. He was brilliant, fascinating, and peculiar. My Christian studies friends regaled me with crazy stories. None was better than his exams and one question in particular: Why?

Why what? Where was he going with this question?

Philosophy is not a multiple-choice class. The study of "knowledge, value, and reason" does not invite the recall of facts. However, how do you answer that question? What is the context? In what direction do you go?

The standard response: Why not?

However, "Why?" is a great question that drills home a critical point. What we do and how we eventually do it are important, but God cares more about why we do them. So why we do things remains a very critical question.

Why does our friend Elly serve families in rural Honduras? Why did she leave Michigan for Central America? Why did God call Elly to serve these families in rural Honduras? Is this her life calling, or is it for a season? We ask why people take risks or escape the routine. These are good questions as we ponder God's direction in our lives and whether we truly stepped out in faith like Elly clearly did.

Moreover, why did the future disciples honor command #2? Why did they leave the life they knew for the unknown and sacrifice everything for the call? And what about the sacrifices they made? For example, biblical scholars believe Peter had a wife and family.

However, what about more traditional career experiences? I have friends who help people invest, balance their money, and file their taxes. I personally guide students in constructing a career vision. Did

God call each of us to these roles? Moreover, for how long and is there a next step? Are we there for a season or longer?

Who we become is most critical to God? So does that mean why we do things is more critical than what we ultimately do or accomplish?

It really comes down to one question. What is our motivation? We can do the right things for all the wrong reasons. You may serve or minister but stop and consider your motive. Is it to further the Kingdom or your own empire? Are you drawing attention to God or your own efforts?

Here is a list of why we choose a specific direction. Which apply to you?

1. Money$$$
2. Fame
3. Acceptance
4. Respect
5. Friends
6. Parents
7. Expectations
8. Insecurities
9. Security

Worldly reasons one and all. Each perfectly understandable, as they flow directly from human nature. No finger-pointing here, as this list includes most every benefit humans desire from life. We work for these reasons, to be honest.

The other options? Eternal. Peter's reason was "because you [Jesus] said so."

Yet these motives move us no closer to God's eternal plan. They offer little insight on whether you are following the right path by using God's GPS. How do you know the path is eternal? That your steps are timeless? Hard to know from your perch.

My calling as a professor includes helping others crystalize their calling, so I have some expertise in this area. Students enjoy access to counseling, mentoring, skill assessments, and aptitude evaluations. Each tool provides valuable guidance in determining a student's "why" in selecting a career. The process can be very logical. Yet responding to a calling runs deeper than that.

Indeed, responding to a calling defies earthly logic. A calling requires us to take uncomfortable steps, those steps that well-meaning friends and family question out of concern for our safety or sanity or both. And we fail in crafting a solid earthly explanation for the providential pivot.

* * * * *

It is truly about connecting why to what and how. The why could be crystal clear, but my experience indicates believers may have, at best, an incomplete understanding of why they are called in a certain direction. Again, God's providence is not a puzzle where we merely lock all the pieces together to reveal a full picture. Some questions are never meant to be answered during this life, which is a gap only faith can fill. That said, sometimes it helps to identify what you know and pray over the blanks. And evaluating where we stand helps with filling in those blanks.

Additionally, God may yet reveal what we are supposed to do specifically and what tools he has provided for our use. These feed into how we accomplish His will.

What does it mean to evaluate something or someone? Here is an example most everyone can relate to at some level. Do you remember the joys of evaluating teachers and professors at semester's end? If you were an A student, it was a chance to extol the instructor's brilliance. But it was a portal of vengeance for all of you C (or worse) students. I know all too well since I have been both.

Professors actually read your comments. Indeed, here is an actual comment made in one of my early course evaluations. I feel comfortable sharing it because I cannot honestly recall whether she meant it as a compliment or an insult. Therefore, no bragging on this end.

"If Dr. Sullivan were an ice cream flavor, he would be mint chocolate chip."

What does that even mean? Granted, a smidge of inductive reasoning tells us mint chocolate chip is an unconventional concoction combining flavors or ingredients that would normally not go together. Presumably, some people believe ice cream flavors shine a light on our psychological profile. One website even noted that fans of this flavor are masters of verbal duels who handle stress calmly. I agree with this analysis.

The student was wise beyond her years. Yet that comment offers zero insight regarding my teaching abilities. And the point of evaluating someone or something is to measure quality based on specific criteria. In fact, evaluating with the wrong criteria is useless.

The point of this book (and your reading it) is to evaluate your career and its alignment with God's calling in your life. Yet a major issue in contemporary Christian life is that those hurdles are typically the criteria we use to measure our own worth and value. I will henceforth refer to those elements as the Providential Paradox, which blocks us from developing a walk with deeper meaning and purpose.

CAKE OR PIE?

Do you like cheesecake? Big fan here. Cheesecake remains an indulgence rarely touching my lips these days, thanks to insatiable health goals. In addition, I prefer key lime pie. This brings us to one of life's immovable existential mysteries: Is cheesecake cake or pie? Might it be something else entirely? How do we resolve such an enigma? Well, we could start by examining characteristics that make cheesecake, well, cheesecake. Cake should go first since it is in the name.

Cake characteristics
- Cake is moist but not wet. Check!
- Cake has texture. Check!
- Cake is consistently the same color. Check!

But what about pie?
- Pie sits on top of crust. Check!
- We bake pie in a pie pan. Check!

This illustration introduces you to the evaluation process. Our purpose lies not in correctly tagging rich, tarty dessert but in breaking down the evaluation process and what it says about our eternal impact.

What does it mean to evaluate something? Here are a few definitions of an evaluation or what evaluating something means:

"Evaluation is a systematic determination of a subject's merit, worth, and significance, using criteria governed by a set of standards."

A more complex definition:

"A systematic determination of a subject's merit, worth, and significance, using criteria governed by a set of standards. ... The primary purpose, in addition to gaining insight into prior or existing initiatives, is to enable reflection and assist in the identification of future change."

Back to simplicity:
- "Judging the value or worth of someone or something."
- Simplicity is your friend.

People evaluate stuff and others formally and informally on a daily basis. Do you want dessert after a great meal? What type? Pie, cake, ice cream? All the above? How do you decide? Which priorities or circumstances do you use to help make the decision?

Here are some possibilities:
1. How hungry are you? Maybe a light snack is on the table, or perhaps you had a fancy meal that left you feeling a little empty that left a hunger void.
2. Are you thinking super rich, sweet, or tart?
3. Are you with other people, and do they want dessert?

These priorities are personal. The evaluation process can be a personal one. What is important to you? We typically commingle our preferences with facts to evaluate effectively.[7] Your next car purchase might skew toward pragmatic over exciting, but certain pesky facts help you identify that tony, mid-priced sedan with great gas mileage. Conversely, horsepower, performance, and style might be critical if you plan to throw pragmatism to the wind.

Such characteristics are called criteria or "a standard on which a judgment or decision may be based," according to the strict dictionary definition.[8] But criteria is simply the characteristics of what you want or tools you can use to determine whether you achieved the desired goal. And criteria remain critical to evaluating people or things. You need good criteria that fit your preferred outcome or goals. I have formally evaluated many ideas or programs during my career.

Here is the process:
1. What do you want (result/criteria)?

---

[7] Granted, another term for personal preferences is bias, which often skews our analysis.
[8] "Criteria." Merriam-Webster.com. 2021. *https://www.merriam-webster.com*. July 17, 2021.

2. What is missing (where you stack up based on criteria)?
3. What is the cost to get it or to get to what you need (can you fill the gap; is it worth it on C/B analysis?) Experts call this process gap analysis. A gap analysis identifies or determines the chasm between where you are and where you need to be, along with the cost required to close the gap. This book follows the gap-analysis model. Our little project identifies where most believers are, where we all need to be, and what it will take to make that trip. This requires a deeper look into the gap-analysis questions.

GAP-ANALYSIS QUESTIONS

1. What do you want or what do you want to happen?
   This touches on the goal or objective you need or want to achieve. This could be transformative or simply making something or someone better. Bottom line, where you want to be once it's all said and done.

2. How do you know you achieved the goal?
   This is where you identify criteria by describing the goal and what it looks like. For example, say you want to be healthier. How would you know if you are moving in the right direction? Well, losing weight, lowering your cholesterol, and being able to work out longer without collapsing are good signs and, thus, criteria. In addition, it definitely helps when you can measure things.

3. What is missing?
   This is where we determine the full extent of the gap. How do you stack up, and what more do you need? This is the true gap analysis. We need a nice roadmap tracing from point A to point Z. You can think of this as a decision-making GPS. We learn how far we need to go and how long it might take to travel the distance from where we are to where we want to be at the end of the process. What will it take, in other words? This phase explains the actual

cost of reaching our goals, which we place next to a list of the benefits. This provides a nice visual when considering the final question for every gap analysis. Individuals and organizations alike must always answer one final question.

4. Is it worth it?
   Do the costs outweigh the benefits? All hopes, dreams, and goals have a cost, and our lot is to decide whether to pay that cost and move forward. Whether one considers a new job, more college, working more, or buying new clothes. Every worthwhile endeavor carries a cost. Granted, God has already decided our calling for us, so our task is merely one of obediently counting the cost and moving forward.

You can use this process for any decision. It works great, provided you have one thing: good criteria. Otherwise, you are going in the wrong direction. Bad criteria make for a bad evaluation because the evaluator is looking for the wrong things. This is the problem with the modern (and especially American) church and the Christian community comprising the church. Contemporary believers march through life looking for the wrong things.

What if we took a moment and ran this through an evaluation process? What would it look like?

WHAT DO PEOPLE WANT?

People struggle with many earthly desires, both carnal and material. Raise your hand if you agree! However, would it be naïve to argue that people ultimately seek meaning and sustainable impact from their existence? In addition, that other stuff merely—and temporarily—populates a giant void. How about we go with that?

How do you know you achieved the goal?

The analysis indicates we achieved a goal by meeting the rigid criteria standards. Recall the health example. The criteria included weight, cholesterol level, BMI, exercise, and diet. These are measurable standards one and all. A middle-aged male (such as myself, sadly!) could target the right numbers to determine whether his health is where it needs to be, or at least improving. Granted, health is a broad, complex subject, but experts accept these criteria as viable indicators of a healthy lifestyle.

That said, what if we chose the wrong criteria. What if I measured my overall fitness based on whether I achieved a new high score or level on one of the many video games my sons devote (waste) hours to playing? How does achieving higher scores, ascending to new levels, or creating new worlds in various video games indicate a person is living a healthy lifestyle? It does not refer to health in any way.[9] What about purchasing gaming computers or sophisticated gaming equipment? Again, zero connection.

The right criteria are critical. The standards must align with the subject or goal. Cool gaming equipment is, well, cool, but it does not help me determine whether I am decreasing my risk of chronic issues or disease. There is nothing inherently wrong with video games, contrary to what most parents tell you.

So what is the proper criteria to determine whether you are aligning your career with God's calling? Table 2.1 includes two sets of criteria based on our Luke 5 subject. Therefore, I titled the list on the left Command #1 Criteria and the list on the right Command #2 Criteria. Most people utilize the Command #1 list to determine the value of their existence.

---

[9] Indeed, one could argue that evidence of excess gaming indicates an unhealthy lifestyle. At least that is my message to teens living in my house. Moreover, they never listen because it would interrupt their game!

Table 2.1
Evaluation Criteria

Command #1 Criteria	*Command #2 Criteria*
Control Live by our plan pursuing goals based on earthly criteria	**Abandonment** Surrender ourselves at the altar of God.
Circumstances Our daily life works to our advantage and paves the road to success and fulfillment. In addition, a little control is nice!	**Faithfully Accept Circumstances** Replace circumstances with understanding that we cannot fully understand where events, both good and bad, take us.
Comparison to Others Life is good provided none of our friends, family, or enemies are doing better than us.	**Count Your Blessings** Circumstances never determine your measure of joy or hope.
Comfort/Security We have our needs met to our satisfaction and in comparison to others.	**Accept Struggles and Even Suffering** Replacing comfort/security with following God means saying goodbye to the comfort zone.
Instant Gratification We consider "needs" met, questions answered, and problems solved on our timeline.	**Compounding Blessings** Replace Instant Gratification with "wait to hear from Him" (waiting without ceasing).

A few thoughts on each standard:

Control

We know what we want but need to pursue what God wants. In addition, frankly, our wants are temporary. Additionally, we struggle with moving forward when circumstances get in the way. Yet we can also surrender ourselves at the altar of God, as explained in the next chapter.

Circumstances

We cannot control circumstances, but they exist for a reason beyond our comprehension or control. Both bad things and good things happen for a reason (as we learn in chapter 4).

Comfort

People like us! We are likeable! Our relationships transcend friction. Replace popularity with God's call for us to take a stand. In addition, you may accomplish Kingdom building that receives little earthly acknowledgment. You may receive scorn even from fellow believers.

Comparison to Others

The comparison trap is the net that ensnares us in a worldly mindset. Comparing simply means identifying the similarities and dissimilarities between two things or people. That definition seems innocent enough. Yet we also know it as the thief of joy—robbing us of joy and diverting our focus from true priorities.

Instant Gratification

We want results! Now please! Yet eternal blessings remain eternal for a reason. **I save this subject for last for a reason!**

Overall, your chosen criteria determines whether you are committed to Kingdom building or empire seeking. You seek a sense of accomplishment in building a career-based legacy. We have done something or created something to hang our hat on in pride. We are without shame or regret. People recall who you were and what you did. Evidence exists. We have done something or created something to hang our hat on in pride. We are without shame or regret. Chapter 7 helps us replace that sense of personal accolades with a "God did this" mindset. Indeed, you might leave a legacy, but it might have little connection with your career and perhaps no link to efforts resulting in compensation—at least your main source of compensation and your career identity.

Are we on the right track with the criteria? Does Command #1 sound familiar? Most people, including believers, hold these standards up as proof their existence is on track. Would you agree? This is where our evaluation goes off the rails because the criteria are all wrong. Look at that list. It certainly meets our worldly needs, but does it accomplish God's plan? Not so much. Yet Christians mark their existence with these benchmarks. I remain as guilty as anyone does in this area. Worldly validation feels good. We sense things are going well.

How do these traits deviate from God's criteria? How can we know we are walking the godly path? What would we evaluate? These traits illuminate why we cannot conduct a gap analysis or count the cost. We cannot finish any evaluation process due to invalid criteria. How can we know if everything is moving in the right direction when our standards create a path moving in the opposite direction? We measure the wrong calculations and collect weak evidence.

Conversely, the right side of the table describes God's eternal criteria under Command #2. So what empirical evidence exists, and how can we know that the second set of criteria rules the day? How about the Bible? Specifically, the giants of the faith. Their lives were built on sacrifice and scorn but ultimately honored by God. And the legacies of the disciples, prophets, and kings were forged in their character rather than marketable skills, although God clearly used those as well. Bottom line: the calling deviated from their plans and their path and interrupted their regularly scheduled programming. They had little say in anything. Yes, this is the criteria we need. Bottom line, eternal criteria yield Kingdom impact while earthly criteria merely build your own, temporary empire. The wrong criteria result in flawed evaluation, which moves you in the opposite direction of God's calling in your life. Consider how a giant of the faith altered his criteria.

Every great fictional story has a great beginning and ending. Our lives leave a legacy with a similar plot. We all have moments where we think about the end. Sometimes things go dark. We hold out hope for safety, but things are in God's hands.

Moments like this lead me to 2 Timothy. This is Paul's goodbye not only to his close friend but also to the ministry and to this world. Paul was on his fourth and final missionary journey, which ended with his second and final prison stint.

Paul felt like a forgotten man. The "so and so has not checked in lately" mentions are here. He also alluded to the shame of incarceration. Yet Paul's faith was unwavering. He counted all shame and worldly scrutiny irrelevant because he cared for everything God entrusted him with during his life.

We know this much about Paul:
1. He cared for who or what God entrusted to him.
2. He maxed out his calling.

What did God entrust under Paul's care? Biblical scholars believe Paul is referring to the many souls his ministry saved over the years. Paul's numerous letters offer us a window into his vision for the flock. Paul envisioned the calling or "career" God planned for him as extending beyond the number of saved souls to preparing those souls to do the same thing—to save others. Therein lies the ultimate objective.

I like this interpretation because I am an outcomes person concerned with what all this effort has actually yielded. I attended a conference once hosted by a political consultant. He started by identifying all the big mistakes campaigns make, whether the candidate is seeking the White House or the job of dogcatcher. The number-one mistake? Candidates, consultants, and volunteers frequently confuse motion with momentum. Everyone assumes being active and sweating means results. Yet all that motion, on its own, is useless. It needs direction.

Paul understood this as well as anyone. The future apostle hailed from the prime commercial center called Tarsus. He expressed pride in his roots. Paul spent his formative years learning from Gamaliel, who was only the most respected religious scholar of the day. This was a mere prelude to Paul's meteoric rise up the Sanhedrin ladder.

He zealously defended his position and beliefs. He was the "chief persecutor" traveling the land to round up followers of "the way." It is fascinating to consider what he gave up in that attic in Damascus. Paul surrendered his prestige, his honor, and his pride.[10]

Paul also surrendered his safety. He snuck out of Damascus quickly. He had come to rely upon the very people he previously sought to punish. He had to convince them he could be trusted.

Humbling.

---

[10] Acts 9:1-19 (ESV)

However, how does Paul become the zealous missionary without these sacrifices? God is (also) in the results business. But those outcomes are not always visible like a ledger or a list of names. Paul's life is a testament to this. God took a respected scholar steeped in the hubris of church leadership and in-dwelled a humility that traveled ten thousand miles by foot for the sake of eternity.

What has God entrusted to your care? Your calling? Your skills or passions? What are the outcomes of all that? I am no theologian, but it seems to me those are the very things God entrusts in our care. These variables establish a career, a legacy. Those and a big ole dash of providence.

And that is what this book is about: developing your eternal legacy!

Paul also maxed out his calling. He did everything God asked, including shedding any sense of comfort or worldly accolades. He traded an exalted position for journeys amounting to ten thousand miles by foot, life-threatening situations, and, ultimately, prison. Paul, more than anything, rejected the status quo that defined his life to spread the gospel beyond the Jewish norm to all nations. God used Paul to achieve an eternal compounding return.

Indeed, responding to a calling defies earthly logic. A calling requires us to take uncomfortable steps, those that well-meaning friends and family members question out of concern for our safety or sanity or both. Moreover, we fail in designing a solid earthly explanation for the providential pivot. That explains why we pursue God's calling. It also explains why we pivot or stay the course. Jesus commanded us to do so, and that will suffice. What do you sacrifice and why? The command calls for sacrificing security and comfort in lieu of risk and uncertainty. Yet we do it because He said so. In addition, God will use you provided your criteria is to achieve eternal alignment. Otherwise, your plan will fail.

As promised, we are moving into the second phase of our journey, as chapters 3-7 compare our earthly criteria with God's standards. We learn that our sense of self-preservation and rugged individualism often betray our calling. The next chapter explores the consequences of going it alone, which include a loss of direction and focus. In addition, our plans look great until something goes wrong. Chapter 3 explores why our own blueprint frequently supersedes God's design.

That said, these five criteria categories speak to personal motive, which is impossible for humans to measure regardless of scientific training. These speak to your "why," as the first paragraph mentioned. Moreover, I posit that internal standards are most critical to God. This was my motivation for writing the book you are currently holding (and hopefully enjoying). Bottom line, God is more concerned about your why than your what. God needs Elly in Honduras, missionaries in the field, pastors in the pulpit, and Paul spreading the message of hope. However, God also needs bankers, lawyers, and accountants. He needs you in your current role and in the future, regardless of your profession, provided your motives are aligned with His criteria.

Perhaps Peter offers the best answer at this point. The gospels of Luke and John describe how Jesus told a group of fishermen led by the soon-to-be-boisterous disciple to "cast their nets over the right side of the boat." Peter agreed to the direction with the added explanation that he did so only because Jesus told him to.[11]

And that explains why we pursue God's calling. It also explains why we pivot or stay the course. Jesus commanded us to do so, and that will suffice. What do you sacrifice and why? The command calls for sacrificing security and comfort in lieu of risk and uncertainty. Yet we do it because He said so. Peter's career pivot was built on this attitude.

---

[11] Luke 5: 4-6; John 21: 6-8 (ESV)

CHAPTER 3
THE ROAD TRAVELED BY GPS

One of the amazing facts regarding the commands structuring our little get-together is how quickly Peter and friends agreed to command number two. What caused the sudden, transformative, life-altering pivot? What divine process guided each one to a clear decision to throw away their means of survival for something eternal? What was their path? We do know they had at least a familiarity with Jesus's message and ministry.

Like the disciples, each of us follows an often-arduous path in carrying out our calling. Faith is a process, or rather a journey. Peter and the apostles started their journey on a lake and ended as exalted martyrs for the faith. This chapter maps out our journey. Ours will almost certainly be less dramatic than Peter's but no less critical.

Maps are fascinating tools. They typically aid in travel or discovery, but they also identify places and clarify proximity. Maps also are a snapshot in time, as urban regions have expanded, leading to the incorporation of the towns on the urban fringe, which we come to call suburbs.

While my love of maps is genuine, I rarely used them back in the day. However, today I use a geographic positioning system (GPS) constantly, even when I know where I am going. I even use it for going to work or getting home. Why? I reside in an urban region, and the commute is unpredictable. Big city living is not for the faint of heart!

Like all technology, GPS transformed our lives. I recall the joy of either depending on a paper map or the well-meaning directions a friend (or stranger) when seeking an unfamiliar destination. "Go left on Brown right after the Circle K!" My favorite? The "you have gone too far" remark. "If you pass the steak house, you have gone too far." This is low-tech "rerouting" for younger readers. Good times!

Granted, these antiquated navigational tools possessed a certain charm, hence the growing map collection. Yet getting from point A to point Z has changed in ways that stun me. My younger self experienced the early phases of the tech revolution, so a "digital map" seemed feasible. I could envision transitioning from the foldable paper map that you could never refold to digitally replicating the routes. Nevertheless, a system that also gives me an ETA plus identifies in advance and adjusts for traffic, accidents, and all manner of delays? I am at a loss for words.

Talking about GPS brings to mind the Christian walk. My normal GPS excursion includes little drama, delay, or distraction. That said, life (and accidents or road construction) happens, especially in Texas, where major highways are in a seemingly eternal "improvement" loop. Such events trigger alternate routes, most of which only slightly deviate from the original path.

However, some deviations are more exotic than others. GPS has rerouted me through a winding, partially paved country road meandering for nearly thirty miles through rural neighborhoods, undeveloped farmland, and two downtowns marked by old courthouses, all to avoid East Texas road construction. This vista bore zero resemblance to the major highway I had been traveling and hoped to one day discover again. Yet the scenic treks are hardly reserved for endless green pastures, as the system has also introduced me to neighborhoods dotting urban enclaves, I would never have known existed save the desire to avoid a twenty-minute delay thanks to a broken-down vehicle up ahead.

Yet GPS typically rescues me from trouble (or traffic) even if it takes me through hairy places or parts unknown. My faith is usually validated. Granted, such short-cuts challenge my trust and faith in the direction-giving voice telling me where to go and when to turn. And I have heard the stories. A couple rigidly sticking to directions ends up in a barren apocalypse miles from civilization. Or, in another case, they missed their hotel check-in time.

Either way, technology is not perfect. GPS is not God, but it makes for a nice providential illustration. Providence via the Holy Spirit takes us in uncharted directions away from the familiar and comfortable. We say goodbye to the interstate and hello to unpaved roads! Still, we cannot control traffic or delays, but GPS can help with those circumstances. However, the solutions may be scary or uncomfortable. Plus, we may not realize the alternative path was the right or best path until our journey concludes.

This chapter takes us on a journey that describes circumstances out of our control and how people respond to said circumstances. We will look at both macro- and micro-level factors. These are events affecting generations, as well as the more personal moments unique to each of us but harboring similar results. Let us compare generations first.

WHAT I LOVE ABOUT GPS!

So how does GPS illustrate the Christian walk/Holy Spirit intercession? How do the technology and mapping guide our literary journey? Perhaps my favorite GPS function can illuminate the connection. GPS gives you options. Drivers receive three possible routes with the best alternative highlighted. The best route is the quickest route, or at least that is the criterion GPS developers chose. I do love the option feature, as my constant goal in life is congestion avoidance!

Yet here is the key: drivers still have a choice. It is our God-given right to choose poorly. You can opt to fight traffic if that is your preference. In addition, my congestion-avoidance goal is not always the right priority if one prefers the quickest route. The app has indicated more than once that my route was the fastest even though it was clearly the most congested. Bottom line, looking for the easiest or safest option with little interference or challenges is not always the best option. Sometimes it is better to face the music and wisely keep moving steadily toward your destination.

That is how GPS illustrates calling. The satellite-driven technology helps us adapt to difficult situations. It also is very simple to follow if you fully trust it. Yet the rub is you can choose a different path. Again, your optimal criterion might deviate from GPS. You also might disagree with GPS and think you know the local roads better than some phone application.[12] Our response is ultimately our own.

OUR RESPONSE

Like the Holy Spirit, GPS cannot make decisions for us. It can influence our response to external pressure or phenomena, but we

---

[12] I have rejected the directions more than once simply because I believed it missed some streets.

possess free will to ignore its advice or guidance. And commuting easily counts as external pressure. How we respond to pressure can determine whether we arrive home safely or cave to road rage.

This chapter leverages the map theme (mapter?) by providing readers directions for navigating this book. What if we examine a more joyous driving experience to illustrate what this chapter brings to the table? My family enjoyed the classic road trip several summers before finally flying to our vacation destination. The longest trip covered two days requiring twenty-two hours behind the wheel! We left home at 4 a.m. on day one to get a good start and arrive at the chosen midpoint at a decent hour. The trip to our destination was exhausting but heading back was a death march! Still, my wife diligently prepared an experience for the boys, including movies, snacks, and games. Her duty was social coordinator. It never felt like a commute to them. (They still rave about our road trips.)

Driving was typically my job. We shared navigational duties. Navigation, especially in a "foreign" land or unfamiliar territory, requires looking for signs. While a road trip is a journey to a desired destination, the trek includes recognizing intervening destinations or signs requiring travelers to alter the travel pattern and proceed in a different direction. Driving any distance eliminates inertia as an option!

My role in our literary road trip includes navigational duties. The next few pages help us identify the intervening topics and signs connecting chapters and our thesis. Additionally, the intervening steps also describe our pursuit of God's calling and the attitudes and priorities (or criteria) that determine whether we reach God's intended destination for our lives.

FOLLOW COMMANDS (HALF BASED ON SELECTED CRITERIA/PRIORITIES)

Like Peter and his fellow anglers, Jesus commands us to follow His will. That is a simple truth. Granted, our journey includes several intervening directions and signs which easily confuse our finite cranial capacity. Indeed, the future disciples received two commands on the lakeshore. Those commands structure our investigation of the thesis and thus our calling. This begins with identifying the criteria for each command. One set keeps our journey and the intervening steps pointed toward the optimal destination, while the other batch leads us astray. Our task involves examining and dissecting each criterion. Indeed, five criteria drive our command choice, which ultimately determines how committed we are to our eternal calling. Each criterion has an opposite criterion from the other list. Chapters 4 through 9 each examine the mirror priorities and the direction they can pull us.

A quick programming note: This does not mean that any instruction from Jesus will lead us down the wrong path. Jesus both commanded and blessed Peter and Andrew when they complied. Again, our response is critical, as is the criteria behind said decision. Will worldly ideals cement our inert tendencies, or do we truly give it all to the Creator? We ponder this question while examining each criterion from both commands.

REAP FRUIT OR EXPERIENCE THE CONSEQUENCES

All decisions carry consequences. Our response to the stimulus, worldly or otherwise, sends us careening in one direction and destiny or another. Science fiction stories often build separate, yet related, worlds or dimensions based on what a character decides. A favorite narrative is when a character experiences competing destinies based on living out the consequences of the various decisions at his or her disposal in a given situation. This book posits that two such dimensions exist—one where we follow God's calling and one where we stick to our own will.

Scripture paints a gruesome portrait, illustrating the many failures of man generally and the Hebrew nation specifically. The Old Testament authors regale us with sins and faithless behavior flowing from royalty as well as the poorest farmers. No one is immune. Jeremiah even remarks on the disgust God experiences when His people turn to idolatry and pagan rituals yet show less commitment to anything other than the pagan groups![13]

God's people suffered for their sins. God removed the hedge of

---

[13] Jer. 7: 16-20 (ESV).

protection for centuries. The people responded with cries for the promised Messiah to save them. Yet the Messiah did not emerge for political salvation. Jesus sacrificed Himself for our sins and rescued believers from eternal bondage.[14]

Believers frequently make this mistake. This is especially true for the American church. Our roadmap labels this command as number one, thinking, *How can our Creator bless this life and us immediately?* Conversely, my purpose in carrying out this project involves building a generation of command number-two Christians willing to sacrifice worldly effects for the Kingdom. Kingdom builders, as opposed to empire seekers, if you will. This requires prescriptive language. I need to discuss how you become a Kingdom builder (see chapter 11).

Readers also need to know whether they are moving in the right direction. My day job includes establishing departmental goals and measurements for determining whether we achieved said goals. People need a progress measuring system, which is why the workbook includes a checklist to measure your commitment to God's criteria.

And that, my friends, is the roadmap. That said, words are nice, but pictures are better.[15] This is the road we will travel together. Again, it serves as an outline for the book but also illustrates the directions your calling can proceed in depending on your response to God's calling.

Paul's journeys covered ten thousand miles as he carried out his missionary work. He spent most of those trips on foot. Paul and his companions sacrificed comfort and safety for the calling. He gave up all the worldly items people crave in order to walk where God needed him.

A final note before moving to the criteria chapters. I need to mention these are internal standards. A serious part of God's plan is pursuing these criteria without fanfare. We live in a "prove it" world that needs empirical evidence to believe something. What is empirical evidence? It is something tangible you can see, touch, or hold. Scientific research relies upon empirical evidence to explain the world and natural occurrences.

We will find that God's calling often avoids empirical evidence. Now, dear readers will quickly retort that Peter enjoyed tangible,

---

[14] Romans 12:2. (ESV).
[15] Book of Acts (ESV).

empirical evidence in the form of nets full of fish. God does operate with empirical evidence. However, that again explains following command number one while blatantly ignoring the second command. Granted, Peter follows Jesus the carpenter's fishing instructions to the letter.

What tangible command number two evidence could Jesus offer? Don't you have questions about any opportunity or really any activity under your consideration? Will the activity prove to be fun, profitable, or enriching depending on the purpose of said action? We typically look for examples of people who benefitted from the activity.

Well, these were the first disciples, so examples will feature people who thrived during or even survived the experience. Peter and his ilk were first responders. Also, what were they getting into in following this Teacher? Yes, Jesus had a huge following, which made an appearance on the banks of Lake Gennesaret. But how did His teachings alter their lives? The fishermen could not answer that question prior to joining the ministry.

Yet Jesus proved He could tend to their basic needs with several full nets as empirical evidence. Jesus spent much of His ministry in fishing communities, yet we know little about this business.[16] We do know a little about professional requirements, licenses, and government intervention. Yet the disciples' work—pre-command number two—remains a bit of a mystery. Still, they obviously trusted Jesus to provide for them and to actually perform their work better than they did!

As promised, we are moving into the second phase of our journey as chapters 4 through 8 compare our earthly criteria with God's standards. We learn that our sense of self-preservation and rugged individualism often betray our calling. The next chapter explores the consequences of going it alone, which include a loss of direction and focus. In addition, our plans look great until something goes wrong. Chapter 4 explores why our own blueprint frequently supersedes God's design.

---

[16] https://www.bibleodyssey.org/en/places/related-articles/fishing-economy-in-the-sea-of-galilee

CHAPTER 4
EVERYONE HAS A PLAN

The world wants us to plan, which does not mean planning is strictly a worldly exercise. The word *plan* appears in scripture 205 times, with many authors extolling the virtues of wise, cautious preparation. Indeed, planning is one of the few topics spanning the breadth of the biblical narrative, with verses spanning Genesis through Revelation.

People smack us with the planning plank early in life. Did my parents throw "fail to plan, plan to fail" in my general direction first? Maybe it was a grandparent, although several buddies reminded me of this edict over the years. Planning remains crucial whether preparing for career, marriage, retirement, or date night at the theater.

So why is planning the first topic among the worldly-criteria chapters? Planning, after all, implies long-term thinking and patience, which are needed virtues we will examine in chapter 7. So what could go wrong? Well, maybe we should review some possibilities out of prudence. Developing our very own calling/career blueprint seems prudent. However, our plans typically last until the first real bump in the road knocks us off course. We simply fail to account for failure or our own human frailties. Yet God's calling shields us from the true impact of our weaknesses and guides us providentially to completing our purpose.

> *"Everyone has a plan until they get punched in the mouth."*
>
> —Iron Mike Tyson, former heavyweight champion

Boxing had never seen a force like Mike Tyson. Is Tyson the best fighter ever to grace the ring? No way. Might he be the most intimidating presence ever to don the gloves? Very possible.

Tyson carried a menacing aura few pugilists can match. Most potential opponents probably hunted for other things to do when anyone mentioned a Tyson match-up. But some fighters and their training team thought they could plan for a pending Tyson meeting. Boxing analysts would regale fans with the dizzying array of skills said foes could utilize to match up against the powerful puncher. Everything from lateral movement to suffocating defense or even the enigmatic "boxing savvy" was heralded as Tyson beaters.

Tyson's response?[17] Well, you already read it. Iron Mike was right, as he recorded fifty wins in fifty-eight career matches. The wins included forty-four knockouts.[18] Fighters accounted for every contingency except being punched in the face so hard recovery is hopeless.

Believers are like that as well. We count on great plans until life punches us in the face. There are big career plans drafted as blueprints for success. There also are family plans that include God's special soul mate.

But then POW! Right in the kisser, as the Three Stooges used to say. A rejection letter arrives from your dream graduate program. Your soul mate breaks off the engagement or rejects your advances before things even reach that point. Perhaps a cataclysmic event occurs, such as divorce, an accident, even the loss of a loved one. The world has a wicked left hook.

Mike Tyson's proclamation begs a critical question. What are we willing to endure? What happens when plans go awry? Do we have a backup plan or an escape route? Do our life and career direction trend downward from lofty plan A to whatever we can get? Or can we persevere? The problem stems from fear but also uncertainty. Are the difficult times part of God's plan for building Christ-like character or a signal to vamoose? Either way, absorbing body blows remains the first example of a hurdle.

You may have also built your blueprint based on bad ideas pursued for all the wrong reasons. We pursue goals for much the same rewards

---

[17] Berardino, Mike. (February 7, 2021). Mike Tyson Explains One of his Most Famous Quotes. *South Florida Sun-Sentinel*. https://www.sun-sentinel.com/sports/fl-xpm-2012-11-09-sfl-mike-tyson-explains-one-of-his-most-famous-quotes-20121109-story.html

[18] Essentially sports. Mike Tyson. May 7, 2021. https://www.essentiallysports.com/tag/mike-tyson/

we sought as tweens and teens. We seek acceptance and exaltation from people who know us or barely know us.

Our childhood continues to haunt us. It's easy to identify the impact on our lives and vision. It is one thing to seek worldly approval, accolades, and huzzahs. That is problematic. But pursuing a direction and priorities based on how we felt or what other people (supposedly) thought about us years ago? What a waste.

Peter had plans for the early church in Acts. It had been a Jewish-centric movement, which worked well until religious leaders stoned Stephen. The movement then spread to the ends of the earth as God always intended. Peter preached to Cornelius, and the Holy Spirit did the rest. Again, God usurped the plans of man for something greater that our tiny brains cannot fathom. And Peter's role expanded beyond his capacity to understand what is possible with God.

Do you do this? I have. Either of the following thoughts indicates the answer is yes:

I will show them!

I hope they fail!

Or, for many of us, pride or shame holds us back.

The impact really cuts much deeper than that. Our childhood haunts us, as it so often is the source of pride and shame. Those wells run as deeply as shale deposits of Texas crude.

Can I share a brief story? A moment in time plays out like so many others at a big airport. Folks arrive to pick up a passenger from a red-eye flight. Said passenger, weary and lethargic, emerges from the paddock to greet friends or family, sacrificing time for a trip to the airport.

But this passenger did not recognize his chauffeurs. He sauntered up to the pair waiting to pick him up and introduced himself.

"Hi, I am Dr. Robert Sullivan."

However, I was on the receiving end of that salutation. This was prior to my adding the PhD credential. Dr. Sullivan, in this instance, was my father, and my sister and I were picking him up from the airport. The only problem was he failed to recognize either of us. (This was a small consequence emerging from his not seeing either of us for over a decade. That and my emerging baldness.)

My family was a mess, as you are seeing. Our father left when I was fourteen. He made appearances from time to time like he was on the speaking circuit. Then dear old dad was a vapor. And yes, it left us with a void.

It also left me with having something to prove. "I will show them!" was my mantra. Success became the void filler. And, of course, I never filled the void no matter what I did.

Who was I trying to impress? Probably those who witnessed my childhood struggles and the lack of a father figure. He made big mistakes. You know what? I am a husband and father who made a few mistakes myself. I can't hold dear old dad accountable for all my challenges.

So what is your void? Whom are you trying to impress? Moreover, does your childhood continue to haunt you? Those early experiences and emotions plant the seed for a life spent chasing an existence built on worldly criteria. We need to identify and root out the bad seeds. Here is a wonderful passage from James to help us accomplish that:

> Come now, you who say, "Today or tomorrow we will go into such and such a town and spend a year there and trade and make a profit"—yet you do not know what tomorrow will bring. What is your life? For you are a mist that appears for a little time and then vanishes. Instead, you ought to say, "If the Lord wills, we will live and do this or that." As it is, you boast in your arrogance. All such boasting is evil. So whoever knows the right thing to do and fails to do it, for him it is sin.[19]

INTRO: OUR PLANS

This is clearly an example of the verses condemning or criticizing the folly of human plans. What is James trying to tell us about the worldly blueprint? Three points stick out in my mind, with all three

---

[19] James 4: 13-17 (ESV).

indicating that the author is more concerned about the foundation and source of our plans than planning.

First, James labels such planning arrogant, but why? And what is the origin of cocky attitudes? Well, the plans are godless by design and echo the command-number-one concerns from chapter 2. The perpetrators tout their own abilities without considering the providential significance and without honoring God's authority and control. Basically, they fail to consider God's plan or even note His providential control of circumstances.[20]

Additionally, the end goal focuses on worldly accolades and wealth. The blueprint ignores eternal consequences. This is a common omission among believers. We supplement personal goals with plans for doing good and carrying out God's plans. We have a binder filled with what I call the "when-thens," to be fulfilled depending on when certain benchmarks are met. "I will give to missions or even pursue a God-based calling to missions when I am blessed with adequate resources to do so." Then I can fully dedicate my life to Christ." Conversely, eternal impact should be the primary focus even though we cannot fully grasp God's calling or outcomes. We cannot predict the future.

This brings us to our final point. The plan and subsequent boasting are future-focused. This point is a little tricky. Indeed, the wording and tone indicate James is arguing mere mortals truly believe they can predict the future! Moreover, there is a little truth to that. Planning obviously assumes a future mindset. What else could we plan for besides the future? I have read several business plans and corporate earnings reports. Fun stuff. Business reports include "forward-facing" language based on projections or business performance predictions, which are based on projections. In fact, the accounting department must indicate in writing that the report includes such language to avoid confusion among investors (or potential investors). Well, plans are forward-facing. Why would James consider that an issue?

We love thinking about and projecting our dreams into a future self with future wealth, success, or recognition. How is this wrong? People derive much of the joy in life from visions of where they can

---

[20] Walvoord, J.F., & Zuck, R.B. (2018). The Bible Knowledge Commentary: *The Epistles*. Easy Sussex, England: David C. Cook.

be or the life their future selves will experience. Frankly, this reality has plusses and minuses. Future projections keep us going, especially during difficult times. And this relies on a factor critical to the human condition: hope. I have frequently heard the cliché "hope is not a plan," which is true. Yet no plan exists without hope. To quote one of my favorite movies: "hope is a good thing. Maybe the best of things." That is true, provided our hope is in the right source. We must assume James would take no issue with this.[21]

What is wrong with planning for the future and harboring hope for the future? Nothing really. Again, the rub is our basis for said hope, dreams, and plans and the criteria that drives those plans.

Of course, we cannot predict the future. Forward-facing language requires a disclaimer for a reason. It could all go south quickly. Sometimes that is for the best. Also, we may not fully appreciate our best-laid plans coming to fruition. The result will most likely look nothing like our future projections.

So how does one design a plan based on God's criteria? We need to master a biblical blueprint. Again, Scripture is rife with planning suggestions and God's promises. Yet we can never go wrong with the Proverbs. Our first source comes from Proverbs 16:3 (ESV):

"Commit your work to the Lord, and your plans will be established."[22]

How does this verse contribute to our blueprint? It truly speaks to every human's desire. People want established plans. According to the Oxford Language dictionary, established items, things, or plans are firm, stable, permanent, and generally accepted.[23] Oh, we would love for our plans to end up like this! Our future hopes and dreams emerge from circumstances and trials to reality. However, the only path to established design is through commitment to the Lord. This requires depending on the grace of God and submitting to eternal wisdom and providence. Rely upon the steady hand of God to weather

---

[21] *The Shawshank Redemption.* Directed by Frank Darabont, performances by Tim Robbins, Morgan Freeman, Bob Gunton, and Clancy Brown, Castle Rock Entertainment, 1994.
[22] *English Standard Version.* (2011). Crossway bibles.
[23] Oxford University Press. 2020. Established. Oxford English Dictionary. https://www.oed.com/

storms, change, shame, or any barrier to our goals. Of course, this also mandates submitting outcomes or results to God and accepting providence whether we like it or not, as well as living with the consequences of our plan actually working.

One more from this timeless book of wisdom: "Many are the plans in the mind of a man, but it is the purpose of the Lord that will stand" (Proverbs 19:21, ESV).

I played one year of college football at a small Baptist university where I accepted Jesus into my heart. We had a senior quarterback/Bible major who eventually went to seminary and pastored a church. He liked to drop this nugget of wisdom on us: "I have not received everything my heart desires. Thank God for that."

Proverbs 19 has God acting as the overruling judge. This aligns with command number 2 from Luke 5. We must not only accept that God's plan overrules ours but that it is the best of all possible outcomes! In addition, His plan can and will break our feeble plans, so appreciate the outcomes while thanking God for the rejection letter.

What does a divine plan look like? What is our blueprint now?[24]

When was the last time you immediately respected someone you just met?

We have brushes with a multitude of people during our lives. The outgoing, humorous folks attract more people and more "likes" since they are more memorable. And I am certainly not disparaging the character of extraverts. Indeed, most people strive toward extraversion, whether at a networking event or taking one of the many personality tests. Extraverts are more popular, as high school taught us.

That said, the quiet, reflective individual is more likely to earn my respect. I call these people "gentle souls." Gentle souls display greater empathy and are not prone to seek attention. They are less likely to leverage social media as a bragging forum. They garner my respect simply because such traits are so rare these days.

My friend Jim is a gentle soul.

This much was apparent when my wife and I met him while attending a new-member orientation class at church. Jim was friendly but also thoughtful and measured in his words. He clearly enjoyed conversing

---

[24] Edit: Summarize via table or graphic.

with other aspiring members at our table with sincere humility.

He has been retired for nearly five years. He prepared for the phase of life in a manner consistent with everything he does, it seems: carefully, incrementally, avoiding the noise. He and his wife are in sound financial shape. However, Jim's retirement goals extend beyond their golden years. They have a personal retirement account (via Jim's 401k) and receive Social Security. That should be adequate.

However, Jim let us know that he had special plans for these funds. "We live off Social Security and devote all resources from the retirement account to ministries. Everything goes to the church and missions. It's called an individual retirement account, but it's really my *eternal* retirement account!"

First, what a testimony! Dedicating more than forty years of income and compounding investment returns to the Kingdom. That gets an amen!

Nevertheless, Jim's commitment got me thinking. The sacrifice truly goes beyond retirement income. They earned money and invested wisely from monthly income for decades. And that monthly salary resulted from daily work. Jim and his wife made daily eternal commitments long before retirement was an option. Their ERA exists because they practiced everyday employment evangelism. They both worked for eternity.

That is what this book is about. Living, working, and planning sacrificially. Just try to create a better blueprint than that!

We have examined factors that challenge our plans in this chapter. We need to see the world in a new way, and we need to see it through God's eternal set of lenses.

How does God see our shame? How does He deal with it?

Well, we know Jesus died for our sins. Paul erases all doubt in Romans: "For the wages of sin is death, but the gift of God is eternal life in Christ Jesus our Lord."[25]

But did Jesus not also die for our shame. Again, we turn to the Apostle Paul and his letter to the Roman church: "[There is] therefore now no condemnation to them which are in Christ Jesus, who walk not after the flesh, but after the Spirit" (Romans 8:1, ESV).

---

[25] Romans 6:23 (ESV).

The book of Romans focuses on the assurance of God's promises. Paul is describing God's nature but also our relationship with Him. He is describing human nature and contrasting it with God's eternal nature. And while Romans 8:1 may directly argue that believers have no condemnation for their sins, we also are protected from our sin nature and the many ways the world would separate us from our Maker.

So escaping shame simply means replacing our big plans with God's big plan. God will carry us when the world hits us in the mouth. He is our enduring power.

And the world does like to hit us in the mouth frequently. What other perils emerge from replacing God's plan with our blueprint?

The remaining chapters in this part of the book address the many punches God helps us avoid. In fact, the next chapter describes the circumstances we must all face.

CHAPTER 5
SHAME AND ITS RESIDUE

Where to begin with Peter and shame-inducing events? We need to address this early in the chapter. The now-revered saint earned the adoration of the ages, but not before earning constructive criticism from Jesus and the frustration of many tasked with spreading the gospel. Frankly, we could spend an entire chapter detailing Peter's shame even with only hitting the lowlights.

Granted, some of the shame-inducing events emerge from Peter (and the other disciples) failing to grasp Jesus's teachings. I think we can all relate to this. For example, Peter struggled to grasp the meaning behind the parable of four soils.[26] He and the other disciples also struggled to understand the "yeast of the Pharisees and Sadducees" lesson, which required Jesus to patiently explain and repeat the phrase.[27] Again, anyone who has sat through a sermon or Sunday school lesson can commiserate with Peter. We all fall short of the wisdom of the ages.

However, theological interpretation could easily have been a source of shame for Peter. His career up to accepting command number two was fishing with minimal if any theological training. While this is conjecture on my part, it is easy to envision Peter mustering up the courage to debate religious leaders steeped in the law.

Peter's other failures draw less sympathy. There was the "suffer the little children to come unto me" moment, where Jesus scolded the disciples for rebuking children who wanted to touch Jesus.[28] Imagine Peter and the other disciples launching into children wanting to see Jesus! It gets worse. In a related "teachable moment," Jesus caught the disciples (with Peter apparently the driving force) arguing over who is the greatest among them, leading to the "first shall be last" denunciation.[29]

---

[26] Matt. 15:16, (ESV).
[27] Matt. 16:1 (ESV).
[28] Mark 10: 13-16 (ESV).
[29] Mark 9: 33-37; Luke 22:24, (ESV).

Some of Peter's transgressions were just weird. The Mount of Transfiguration conversation between Jesus, Moses, and Elijah is a prime example. Peter is there along with James and John, but none of the disciples are part of the conversation, and no one is addressing Peter directly. Still, he simply could not help himself and noted that it was good the three disciples were there to build shelter for the three saints.[30]

While we can make light of a few blunders, many of Peter's missteps could have or outright did hurt the movement. He spoke for Jesus when asked whether the Teacher would pay the two-drachma temple tax, which spurred Jesus to put Peter's fishing expertise to good use as the disciple caught a four-drachma-carrying fish.[31] The fish saved the day, but Peter placed Jesus in a bad situation given His preaching against what the temple had become thanks to greed and the Roman Empire.[32]

And then there are the big failures. Falling asleep in the Garden of Gethsemane at perhaps the most historically inopportune time ever.[33] Rejecting Jesus's explanation of the coming crucifixion and ascension, leading Jesus to exclaim, "Get Thee behind me Satan!" for only the second recorded instance. The other time He was actually speaking to Satan, so Peter clearly messed up.[34] The post-ascension Peter was also not immune to foibles, including distancing from Paul and the uncircumcised Gentiles when the Pharisees came for a visit.[35]

Finally, denying his affiliation with Jesus three times in one night remains Peter's most bitter shame pill to swallow. It fulfilled prophecy, for one. The denials also exposed Peter's spiritual and physical weakness. He struggled to overcome this lapse.[36]

These blunders apparently filled Peter with shame almost beyond recovery. He went back to fishing temporarily until Jesus lovingly reinstated him.

---

[30] Mark 9:5, (ESV).
[31] Thus providing for both Jesus's and Peter's temple tax.
[32] John 2: 13-25 (ESV).
[33] Mark 14-32-42; Matthew 26: 36-56 (ESV).
[34] Matthew 16: 21-28 (ESV).
[35] Galatians 2:11 (ESV).
[36] Matthew 26:74 (ESV).

> When they had finished eating, Jesus said to Simon Peter, "Simon son of John, do you love me more than these?"
> "Yes, Lord," he said, "you know that I love you."
> Jesus said, "Feed my lambs."
> Again Jesus said, "Simon son of John, do you love me?"
> He answered, "Yes, Lord, you know that I love you."
> Jesus said, "Take care of my sheep."
> The third time he said to him, "Simon son of John, do you love me?"
> Peter was hurt because Jesus asked him the third time, "Do you love me?" He said, "Lord, you know all things; you know that I love you."
> Jesus said, "Feed my sheep. Very truly I tell you, when you were younger you dressed yourself and went where you wanted; but when you are old you will stretch out your hands, and someone else will dress you and lead you where you do not want to go." Jesus said this to indicate the kind of death by which Peter would glorify God. Then he said to him, "Follow me!"[37]

Can you imagine letting Jesus down? Well, we do it all the time, just like Peter. Yet what we envision as barriers to a relationship with our Creator are often open doors if we focus on God's strength and love over our own weakness.

"I am getting new hearing aids!"

Lea was beside herself. She had just left the audiologist's office with the good news. A hearing-aid producer had recently developed a smaller, lighter hearing aid. And she was using them during our phone call! We quickly scheduled a coffee-and-snack rendezvous so I

---

[37] John 21: 15-19 (ESV).

could see the little miracles.

This was roughly the six-month point of our relationship, which had been built upon almost five months of friendship. I knew from the first moment Lea spoke that she was hearing impaired. Indeed, she detailed the story early in our acquaintance. The hearing loss stemmed from a birth defect, yet her parents and doctors didn't realize that Lea had profound hearing loss until after she turned three. Speaking of misses, Lea is a twin, and no one had any idea of her existence until delivery day. Born two minutes after her sister, the little four-pound newborn was clinging to life for nearly a week and did not go home for three weeks.

Lea was definitely a miracle, but the trauma left a mark. A babysitter was keeping the twins when a lamp fell a few feet from where they were playing. Beth, Lea's "bigger" sister, jumped and screamed like most scared kiddoes. Lea kept playing, oblivious to the noise and shattered lamp. An audiology test reinforced the logical conclusion. Lea had profound hearing loss, which meant she was without 90 percent of normal hearing capacity.

But that never stopped her. The Lea I knew was energetic, athletic, and beyond capable. Lea lived independently in a big, urban enclave. She never shied away from a challenge and communicated via lip reading with a little help from the hearing aids.

I was quite impressed. Frankly, Lea's perseverance and resilience were some of her most attractive characteristics. This meant I found the need for those characteristics, namely her hearing loss, an attractive aspect as well.

Nevertheless, back to coffee. Once we arrived and settled down with our drinks, Lea unveiled the new hearing aids, which were radically different from the traditional version. Most readers are aware of the typical hearing aid model. A brown speaker tucked behind the ear lobe connected to an inner ear mold by a transparent tube. The new one looked nothing like that. They looked like shriveled red peppers that fit right in your ears. Hidden in the ear and invisible to the eye.

And that is why she liked them. But I digress.

I was happy for Lea. Yet I pondered her excitement level. Why was getting new types of hearing aids such a big deal? My answer came soon enough.

Lea called me again twenty-four hours later. She was in tears. The final test called for wearing the hearing aids for a few days, including at work, before Lea fully migrated to the new option. All seemed well until a well-meaning coworker pulled Lea aside to inform her that the aids would not stop ringing. This indicated that Lea had the volume increased beyond the unit's capacity. The smaller hearing aids simply did not possess power adequate to address her hearing loss.

The audiologist confirmed that Lea would need to use the older version, and she was not taking it well. I rushed to her apartment to provide comfort. She explained the office incident through her weeping. I listened compassionately but finally asked gently why the new hearing aids were so important to her. The answer provided a deeper understanding into her experiences and trials.

Lea described the challenges she faced. Kids making fun of her voice. Staying home with her parents while friends went out with their boyfriends. People asking her what country she was from because they thought she had an accent.

Lea summed it all up: "I always felt like the ugly deaf girl and wanted to be something different for you."

And just like that, my heart melted. Everything that impressed me about her brought her pain. Everything I found attractive and strong brought her shame. I doubt this comes as a big shock, but I married Lea and she remains the kindest, most loving and patient person I know. She is an awesome wife, teacher, and mother for our two boys. Lea grappled with shame and emerged victorious, but she would tell you it was only through God's intervention and help.

These factors cause us to flinch in certain situations:
- Events and experiences from the past.
- Individual struggles and failures.
- What people think of you or what you perceive them to think of you.
- Shame in its many forms.

Shame is not like guilt. It is inwardly focused and perhaps a bit selfish, if we are being honest.

Some people wear it like a disgraceful badge, while others hide it with charm, hard work, or some other cloaking device. The shame affect is odd because it can either hinder people or drive them to greater heights. Granted, some heights are not safe or healthy. And the shame-driven brand typically (but not always!) emerges from command number-one criteria. So as always, our concern in this chapter is not merely how shame barricades you from worldly success, but what type of success it may propel you toward and the harm that may come of it.

A good friend once argued that we never really leave middle school. His point was that people essentially drift through mature life tethered by the same motives, fears, and general hang-ups as our younger versions.

What does this mean? Here is a short list describing middle school life and its impact on our brains
1. You are focused on what people think about you.
2. You respond to input with hyperbole.
3. You seek an exclusive group of friends.
4. You hope your group is part of the "in-crowd."
5. Sometimes to the exclusion of others. (This is not always done in a mean way.)
6. You crave approval.
7. You fear the world will never recognize your unique significance and what makes you special.

Basically, people's opinions of your actions, beliefs, and style still mean everything. You reward constructive criticism or well-meaning ideas with sarcasm or even anger. You zealously pursue access to the "in-crowd," even if that means choosing a certain Sunday school class or even a church. You make friends with people partially due to their access to the favored crowd. You eventually disconnect from others, perhaps due to this focus. Validation and recognition are critical.

WHAT COULD GO WRONG

The list strikes me as hit and miss. Some of these are accurate and at times pervasive, while others miss the mark. Still, my buddy has a point. I join him in believing that our childhood haunts us. We carry early scars with us whether we see them or not. Why do those early scars cut more deeply?

Get away from there!

Nothing said summer like picking blackberries with Mimy in mid-June. This meant enjoying her award-winning blackberries (with ice cream) after consuming a home-cooked, stick-to-your-ribs feast. The feast typically featured homemade chicken-fried steak, cornbread, and veggies straight from her garden. This was no personal, urban garden but a country garden that stretched a good twenty yards lined with taters, tomaters, black-eyed peas, corn, and squash. I always had blackberry-picking and pea-shelling duty. And eating, of course. It was heavenly, at least until the bellyache hit!

Yet pulling blackberries sometimes proved more treacherous than it sounds. Turns out snakes like blackberries too. Mimy and I ran into a small reptile that looked venomous to our untrained eyes.

Mimy was eighty-three, and she held no fear when it came to snakes. Killing the critters was routine. Just ask me about the time she used her hoe to pummel a chicken snake scheming to abscond with the chickens' eggs.

But I did not inherit her fearlessness. My eight-year-old self made a beeline back to the house. Mimy followed closely behind, and we both peered out the screened-porch door as a tiny baby black snake slithered away from our treasured blackberries.

It really was a baby. However, Mimy, perhaps sensing a little shame, took stock of the gravity of the situation. "Good thing we got out of there! You know, the little ones use all their venom when they bite you. They cannot control it like the big ones!"

This observation hung with me all these years. I assumed it was true because other people say the same thing. Indeed, I was watching a YouTube video with a park ranger holding a baby water moccasin while warning everyone the little ones are more dangerous since they use all their venom, yada, yada. You probably stopped reading past "holding a baby water moccasin," and I cannot blame you!

Anyway, my endless curiosity drove me to dig a little deeper on the topic of snakes and their baby venom. Turns out the science is at best "inconclusive," with few herpetologists endeavoring to compare bite toxicity between parent vipers and their offspring. So maybe Mimy was right and it is just a myth. I would avoid holding them either way.

Yet we can safely note that little humans expel all their venom on others. Whether it be middle-school kids practicing exclusionary seating on the bus or the cafeteria, groups of teenagers picking at a weak victim, or simply ostracizing outsiders or anyone who dresses slightly differently, youth often aim for the heart and rarely miss.

Granted, it may just seem that way due to our vulnerable nature at this formative life stage. Moments both good and wretched will clearly stick longer than a similar experience in middle age. Still, I can clearly recall references to parents getting divorced, poor families, general hygiene, physical shape and athleticism, and intellect. Everything was on the table except pulling punches. Some of those comments were as memorable as blackberry cobbler.

Those comments bite, with the passage of time only partially healing the wounds. It is sad that part of our life can be wasted on comments made decades ago. Our nature makes it difficult to forget and move forward cleanly.

Sometimes those shots come early. The world knocks some folks down before they have a chance to get rolling. A family friend was a mere twelve years old when her family was in a horrific car accident that claimed the life of a pedestrian. This remains the most traumatic event in her life.

The aftermath was difficult, as you would expect. The victim's family was beyond gracious in reaching out. Yet the pain lingered. Every family member received counseling with a specific focus on the psychological well-being of the children. Time and grace eventually brought healing.

Yet the impact lingers. Our friend still experiences sudden reflex responses to shadows and peripheral images when driving, coupled with the occasional flinch from oncoming traffic. These all remain from an accident that took place during her tween years.

Chaotic or cataclysmic events leave a residue that colors our response to the world, whether we are talking about reflex or reflective actions. Have you dealt with trauma? I refer to moments without warning, such as my wife's accident, as well as events that unfold over time. They are hard to shake. Grown children reconsidering marriage due to their parent's divorce immediately pops into my head. Such events can also separate you from God or at least hurt the relationship. They can also draw you closer.

They also cause us to flinch, like Lea. Maybe not from oncoming traffic but possibly increased responsibility, job changes, or criticism. Events or things people said years ago still alter our follow-through.

Yet so do less dramatic run-ins with the world. Circumstances colluding or colliding to withhold our hopes and dreams. The allegedly well-meaning critiques from teachers or coaches. Even comments with uplifting intentions often leave a mark.

I heard a professional counselor speak on the topic of shame. He said one of the most damaging comments his parents leveled at him during the formative years was that he was "hard-working" compared to his brothers. His interpretation? His parents were indicating he worked harder because he had to, as his intellectual capacity paled in comparison to his siblings. This residue stuck well past college.

Shame happens when we let the world—rather than God—tell us who we are. And shame leaves residue, especially early shame. Our childhood haunts us but also shapes us. I teach the concept of political socialization. Socialization is the process by which we understand the world and our role in it. My approach in teaching the concept is to hand each student a clear transparency sheet and magic marker. I ask each student to write the following on the clear sheet:

- People you knew who influenced you.
- Major events that changed you.
- Personal moments or experiences.
- Popular culture you consumed that was formative.

Then I tell them to cover their face with the sheet. This is your vision! How you see the world and your place in it, including feedback both positive and painful.

This is socialization, the process of how you form your view of the world. The early events build drawers (or Google drives!) of filing folders where you deposit experiences and thoughts. The early years categorize everything. We call them formative years for a reason. We struggle to break away from this structure.

This explains personal shame as everyone confronts his or her personal barriers. That said, macro circumstances can affect how entire generations view calling and career. Those of you dear readers in the tender Millennial-Gen Z range, you see the world differently than we older folks because, well, your world is different from ours. At least the one we grew up in as well as the ones our parents experienced.

My parents were part of the baby boomer generation. The baby boom moniker alludes to the unprecedented number of births during the eighteen-year span from 1946-to 1964. Post-war couples wanted to start building families.[38]

And build families was what they did. Seventy-seven million babies were born, accounting for forty percent of the American population at the time. This was not limited to the United States.

The birth rate creates such a large bulge on any chart that demographers refer to this as the "pig in a python" generation. And the impact remains powerful and evident given the boomer birth explosion coupled with that same generation's hitting the reproductive brakes. It still comprises nearly 22 percent of the American population, placing it second behind millennials. This coupled with increased age expectancy leaves the boomers in a critical market position that plays no small role in transforming how we perceive retirement.

The baby boomers' career experience deviated from previous workers in a radical manner. College morphed from elite to affordable to a credential-delivering commodity necessary for upward mobility or middle-class entry. Yet the hissy fit mentioned earlier created diversions. Practical majors gave way to idealistic degrees designed to broaden the learners' life vision.

Radical young lives of boomers typically gave way to a normal state remarkably similar to their parents' lives, with a few tweaks. Boomers fed up with large families produced smaller families. In addition, the suburban experiment continued with new towns replacing aging suburbs.

This era included economic upheaval. It was real and not very fun. Frankly, boomers received a gift from their parents called inflation. Like many countries, the American federal government spent exorbitantly to "prime the pump" and put a charge into the economy. The plan was awesome until prices skyrocketed amid double-digit inflation. In fact, for boomers, the late seventies delivered a double body blow of inflation and economic recession.

This combo even hit home with preteen (tween?) me. Gas prices zoomed to almost seventy-nine cents per gallon in a matter of weeks. Yes, seventy-nine cents! That was triple the normal rate of twenty-five cents per gallon. Imagine current prices tripling to nine dollars! This led

---

[38] Dimock, M. (2019, January 7). Defining Generations: Where Millennials End and Generation Z Begins. Pew Research Center. *https://www.pewresearch.org/fact-tank/2019/01/17/where-millennials-end-and-generation-z-begins/*

to actual gas lines where you could fill up only on certain days based on certain criteria. In Waco, Texas, the standard was the motorist's last name. You could pump gas on Monday and Wednesday if your last name started with A through L, or Tuesday and Thursday if M through Z. The lines stretched for miles.[39]

I remember waiting in line for thirty minutes one Wednesday evening only to coast home on fumes because my dear mother got the schedule confused. I hate to sound like your grandpa, but this was before cell phones. We were minutes from pushing the family Oldsmobile home. These memories clouded the baby boomer years and the perception for the next generation.

People born during the years 1965–1980 comprise Generation X. This was an odd time to grow up, frankly. It threads the needle from the counterculture, hippy years to the Reagan years, also known as the dawn of the modern conservative era.[40]

Would you indulge me as I relate one more story? I loved watching cartoons with my boys when they were little. We binged for hours on *Phineas and Ferb* or *Gravity Falls,* spawning great memories and laughs. I finally introduced them to some of the formative cartoons from my youth.

This was a weird time to grow up. Watch a seventies TV show. Everything is in a unique time capsule set partly in a different dimension: the hair, the clothes, the furniture, and the curtains. Yes, every decade develops a unique style or mark, but this decade stands alone in many ways.

This worldview proved inescapable for a child until forces both political and cultural blew it all away. Some political leaders impact public policy in ways seen and unseen, while others transform the entire culture through the cult of personality. Ronald Reagan was the latter and his election ushered in a generation of young capitalists whose

---

[39] Siegel, J.J. (1994). *Stocks for the Long Run: The definitive guide to financial markets & long-term investment strategies.* Chicago: McGraw-Hill.

[40] Strzemien, A. (2019 May 14). *Gen X is a Mess.* The New York Times, Style.

sole goal was wealth accumulation and conspicuous consumption.[41] I am not afraid to say my generation prioritized greed and what was happening on the surface over substance.

The culture mimicked (and at times mocked) these priorities. Like the seventies, the eighties carried a definite vibe that is easy to spot. Both eras were loud, but the eighties were loud in an uptight, "look at me!" fashion. Less security and comfort and more world domination, or at least domination of your little world.[42]

The economic experience drove this as a bumpy ride with little hope for security. The older Xers majored in big-money education as the stock market and economy exploded. MBAs and JDs became the rage, as wealth accrual remained the goal. Then as the credential-gathering came to an end, so did the good times.[43]

The early nineties. Sigh. A crippling recession arrived just as the generation was ready to apply that knowledge to the work world and capture their piece of the action.[44] Yet this morphed into a brief pause as the markets roared during the latter half of the decade. Eight surging years driven by the earliest e-commerce phase. The wheels came off again in 2001 as investors realized either companies with massive stock prices made no money or their accountants pretended they did.[45] Again, this was merely a brief pause as market forces pushed wealth to higher levels.

Then 2008 happened. Words escape me. The greed/crony industrial complex yielded a massive real estate bubble that rightly should have produced another depression save government intervention.[46]

Bottom line, the Gen X economic metaphor is less a roller coaster and more a flight where the pilots avoid crashing right before the plane nosedives to the earth before ascending beyond forty thousand feet to the heavenly skies. Except this happened four times over the course of a

---

[41] Hayward, S.F. (2009). *The Age of Reagan: The conservative counterrevolution: 1980-1989.* New York: Three Rivers Press.
[42] Strzeman, 2019.
[43] Hayward, 2009.
[44] Hayward, 2009.
[45] McLean, B. & Elkind, P. (2013). *The Smartest Guys in the Room: The Amazing Rise and Scandalous Fall of Enron.* New York: Penguin.
[46] Sorkin, A.R. (2010). *Too Big to Fail: The Inside Story of How Wall Street and Washington Fought to Save the Financial System—and Themselves.* New York: Penguin books.

five-hour leg. Everyone lived and made it home, but Amtrak suddenly had a new set of customers.

This generation put a unique spin on the American dream. Bargain bin interest rates begat bigger mega homes in new, shiny, McMansion-filled suburbs extending ever farther from the urban core but still in its stratosphere. They had more children on average than boomers, as millennials and Gen Z are larger. It all seemed filled with secure confidence on the surface, but everyone acknowledged the recession bogeyman was right around the corner, and his shadow seemed to loom larger every time. Therefore, get your own ducks in a row because no one will do it for you.

This is especially true for retirement planning. Gen X is the first group solely dependent upon leveraging self-directed retirement products such as the 401k or IRA to achieve solvent golden years, as opposed to an employer-funded and defined pension. Social security is hardly a given, thanks to the boomers' size. It leaves people feeling squeezed at times.[47]

Perhaps this should have been predictable. The boomers who ushered in Me-ism produced this generation that came of age as wealth expanded. Additionally, whether it be due to excess greed or government miscues, what economically goes up always plummets. It can leave someone a bit squeamish.

These are "corporate" circumstances shared by generations. A connective tissue binding everyone born in a specific range of years or decades. However, we each carry our own circumstances that either bolster our fortunes or place barriers in the life map we created to ensure a fulfilling, successful life envied by others. This typically leaves us with decisions to make (stay the course vs. a new direction), although sometimes there is no decision to make. God has spoken. People often view these moments as compromise windows where they transition hopes downward from lofty Plan A to Plan B or even C.

However, is that really happening? Does God have perhaps even bigger plans?

The list of biblical figures whose faith transcended difficult or trying

---

[47] Rae, D. (2021). 9 Ways Gen-X Can Get on Track for Retirement. Forbes. *https://www.forbes.com/sites/davidrae/2021/03/21/9-ways-gen-x-can-get-on-track-for-retirement/?sh=2788016f3395*

circumstances is lengthy. Frankly, this is really the biblical narrative. God saving us from ourselves is the very definition of mercy, and giving us what we do not deserve defines grace. Every sacred story includes one of both elements, which means I pick one. You might pick a different person, and that is okay. We can agree to disagree. Certainly, Paul, Joseph, David, or even Jonah would fit the bill, but my goal is to offer a more obscure yet important example, which brings us to Mordecai. Mordecai is a critical figure in the book of Esther. Indeed, while Esther is the book's title, Mordecai is as much a protagonist. Esther is a weird yet oddly endearing Old Testament Scripture. It is the only book in the Bible with zero references to God, but His presence is throughout the story as if He is orchestrating circumstances and coincidences behind the scenes. I love the book for that very reason: that is truly how God operates from our perspective.[48]

The setting is unique. Several members of the Hebrew nation return to Jerusalem during the era Esther details to reestablish temple worship via Mosaic Law. However, some (like Esther and Mordecai) stayed behind in Susa, the capital of Persia, leading to the assumption by some biblical scholars that they were more secular.

Like other figures, Mordecai had a nice situation, all things considered. He enjoyed a prominent role in King Xerxes' court during the Hebrew exile, perhaps due to his cousin Esther ascending to the queen's throne. Yet the circumstances elevating both Esther and Mordecai threatened not only their lives but also the very existence of the exiled Jewish community. Mordecai refused to bow to Haman, Xerxes' principal minister. Haman responded by not only plotting to have Mordecai killed but also to bring about the complete eradication of the Jewish population with Xerxes' approval. Yet Mordecai and Esther thwarted the attempted genocide through courage, faith, and divine intervention, even though the author never references God. In fact, Xerxes called upon the Hebrew nation to defend itself against its oppressors, which they were more than happy to oblige.[49]

Our circumstances were never quite so dire, but we struggle with having zero control over the circumstances surrounding our existence.

---

[48] *Esther.* (1995). Matthew Henry's New Testament commentary. London: Hodder & Stoughton
[49] Book of Esther (ESV)

Cultural and economic upheaval color every generation, especially during the early formative years. Like Mordecai, believers must refuse to bow before the world. Of course, circumstances are external events or situations of a particular time and place. Believers also encounter internal barriers that seem to permanently bar God's mercy.

Shame and its twin, pride, are harbingers of quiet destruction. Chapter 6 discusses the very human (and American) tendency to compare our lives and their output to others. The need for worldly validation sets what I refer to as the comparison trap, which eventually ensnares all of us at some point. And this trap is truly deadly as no outcome offers eternal benefits.

CHAPTER 6
THE COMPARISON TRAP: KEEPING UP WITH AND COMPETING AGAINST THE WORLD

Can I start this chapter with a little humblebrag? I want to show you a little gift I got from a coworker and friend. It's a ten-million-dollar bill. The most expensive gift anyone has bestowed upon me.

So many questions must be flowing through your mind:

What if you used the bill for something like coffee or breakfast? Imagine running into your local convenience store and laying this down?

How do you break a ten-million-dollar bill? Clerks usually lose it over one-hundred-dollar bills.

How long would it take to count out the change?

Where would you put the change? It wouldn't fit in a wallet, and it would take a whopper of a purse.

ZIMBABWE INFLATION

Luckily (or unluckily), none of that is an issue with this particular note. The African nation of Zimbabwe issued it. So maybe a relocation would ensure my life of affluence. But it wouldn't because a currency-exchange analysis told me this bill's exchange rate with the U.S. dollar is four cents.

I could trade in this baby for four American pennies. But it's a nice shade of red.

Zimbabwe is known for runaway hyperinflation. You were promised no math, but bear with me for mere illustration purposes. The U.S. economy historically averages an annual inflation rate of 3 percent.

Zimbabwe's rate of inflation? 100,000%.[50] That is not a typo.

Let us seek to understand what this means in the real world. How long would it take for the price of things we need to double given these inflationary rates? To help answer that, let's check on the rule of seventy-two from chapter 1. The United States rate is straightforward. Dividing seventy-two by three leaves us with twenty-four years for food, cars, and homes to double in price. We can manage that.

The academic definition of inflation is "a general increase in prices and fall in the purchasing value of money."[51] So every item you need to purchase costs (a little bit) more. This is natural and expected in a stable country with decent economic growth. Most people are working while some people are making more than they did in the past, which means there is more money to spend.

However, the Zimbabwe experience is anything but normal. It offers a case study in artificial inflation. Government activity such as issuing more debt or increasing the amount of currency artificially increases prices. The rule of seventy-two in this instance predicts that prices double several times daily. This means my exalted G note might yield a bus ticket downtown, but the trip home would set me back $20,000,000

This economics lesson illustrates two concepts:

The rule explains compounding blessings but also compounding burdens such as inflation and interest owed. Likewise, our calling can yield compounding burdens as well as compounding blessings. The barriers build up over time if left ignored.

The rule initially explained how much money you reap from long-term investing. However, it also identifies how much it costs to borrow money plus the impact of inflation on your hard-earned ducats. Your relationship and attitudes toward money typically seal your fate. My friend Jim developed a healthy monetary mindset, which resulted in positive compounding. This is hardly the American norm. We crave conspicuous consumption of goods and services that help us feel

---

[50] International Monetary Fund. *Inflation Rate, Average Consumer Prices.* Accessed May 19, 2021. *https://www.imf.org/external/datamapper/PCPIPCH@WEO/OEMDC*

[51] "Inflation." *Merriam-Webster.com. http://www.merriam-webster.com.* (October 13, 2021).

wealthy but, more importantly, create an affluent image that demands respect and awe from friends, family, and the world at large. This segues to point number two.

Worldly validation is a form of artificial inflation. Earthly success is inadequate on its own terms. We need validation from others. We want people to know and acknowledge our accomplishments. I call it artificial validation or AV, given its fleeting and destructive nature. And what is the AV medium? Why social media, of course!

Facebook is the case study. Look at our vacation and all the fun parties with beautiful friends. No worries here! Yet blaming social media almost has a hollow "shoot the messenger" feel to it. Social media simply shines a light on the human condition. We advertise our ideal brand to the world because we want everyone to see that while reality remains much murkier. Social media is merely the portal for our insecurities. Your life becomes a search for consumption over meaning.

Have you ever heard of a Veblen good? Veblen goods are status-symbol purchases. The more outlandishly expensive, the better. Identify any product with zero utility other than "keeping up appearances"—luxury cars, jewelry, wine, designer clothing. Economists call this the "snob effect." Indeed, the Veblen effect occurs when people buy luxury items when perfectly viable, less expensive options of the same product exist. Think of your friends who acquire BMWs or Mercedes when a Honda or Toyota is just as reliable.[52]

This reminds me of our young parenting years. Several expectant couples spent egregious amounts of money preparing for the blessed day. Baby clothes from Nordstrom's and Neiman-Marcus, cribs from boutique stores costing three times the price of normal cribs. My inquiries over the conspicuous purchases always received the same response: "Only the best for the baby!"

Okay. Those designer onesies lasted maybe a week. The cribs were no safer than retail brands. How did this help the baby? Or did it allow the parents to maintain a certain standard? I know first-hand those designer diapers ended up in the same place as our grocery store brand and with the same contents! Frankly, poop is poop regardless of the cost of the container.

---

[52] Veblen, T. (1899). *The Theory of the Leisure Class.* Macmillan.

And one burden (maybe even curse) we bear is the burden of comparing.

Social media is also the comparison portal. We need benchmarks in life. Happiness or success occurs relative to the happiness and success of others. Am I really maximizing my existence if the level three acquaintance I friend on Facebook has a more killer life?

Or put another way, we compare how the world views us and worships others.

Peter and the other disciples struggled with comparison. Peter, after all, was part of the apostolic inner circle along with James and John. He almost assuredly believed himself to be one of the chosen among the chosen. They were the Mount of Transfiguration triumvirate!

Have you ever been blessed with great responsibility? Perhaps the captain of the football team, volleyball squad, or the theatrical lead. You may have been president of some organization or your school. I had several opportunities carrying heavy burdens. Such challenges bring us into close proximity with important people. While the stress is exhausting at times, power can be intoxicating. Some of the disciples clearly struggled with humbly accepting the authority and responsibility Jesus delegated.

Do you have friends or acquaintances who spend most of their time talking about themselves? It is maddening! I always try to pivot to a different topic, but they will always find a way to bring it back to them. Anyway, Jesus is dealing with twelve me-centric individuals comparing their status with the most important figure they knew. This hopefully dispels any notion that Facebook and social media are responsible for the comparison trap. Peter's needed a benchmark, and it was how Jesus viewed his importance relative to the other eleven disciples.

Our benchmark is how does the world view us compared to others? Do we receive adulation in equal or greater measure? Will people recognize or remember us?

This mindset poisons our walk as few other thoughts can. You will experience brain rot as you allow yourself to be vexed over why Bill has a better job or Frank has a larger house. Or why Marge keeps ascending the ladder and absorbing favor even though she is a poster child for corruption.

A Psalmist penned his tales of comparison woe for the historical record. Asaph was a prominent singer in King David's court who also served as a chief Levite minister. That said, Asaph's most enduring legacy was drafting several Psalms at the king's behest.

Psalm 73 is one of Asaph's most exalted compositions. It offers us a wonderful peek inside his battle with envy and temptation.[53] Indeed, the first twenty verses describe how he fell into those traps and how he escaped.

> Truly God is good to Israel,
> to those who are pure in heart.
> But as for me, my feet had almost stumbled,
> my steps had nearly slipped.
> For I was envious of the arrogant
> when I saw the prosperity of the wicked.
> For they have no pangs until death;
> their bodies are fat and sleek.
> They are not in trouble as others are;
> they are not stricken like the rest of mankind.
> Therefore pride is their necklace;
> violence covers them as a garment.
> Their eyes swell out through fatness;
> their hearts overflow with follies.
> They scoff and speak with malice;
> loftily they threaten oppression.
> They set their mouths against the heavens,
> and their tongue struts through the earth.
> Therefore his people turn back to them,
> and find no fault in them.
> And they say, "How can God know?
> Is there knowledge in the Most High?"
> Behold, these are the wicked;
> always at ease, they increase in riches.
> All in vain have I kept my heart clean

---

[53] Walvoord, J.F., & Zuck, R.B. (2018). *The Bible Knowledge Commentary: Law.* Easy Sussex, England: David C. Cook.

and washed my hands in innocence.
For all the day long I have been stricken
And rebuked every morning.
If I had said, "I will speak thus,"
I would have betrayed the generation of your children.
But when I thought how to understand this,
it seemed to me a wearisome task,
until I went into the sanctuary of God;
then I discerned their end.

Truly you set them in slippery places;
you make them fall to ruin.
How they are destroyed in a moment,
swept away utterly by terrors!
Like a dream when one awakes,
O Lord, when you rouse yourself, you despise them as phantoms.
When my soul was embittered,
when I was pricked in heart,
I was brutish and ignorant;
I was like a beast toward you.
Nevertheless, I am continually with you;
You hold my right hand.[54] (Psalm 73:1-23, ESV).

Asaph starts by describing how he came to envy the wicked, which resulted in his temptation. The envy tripped him up. He glories in the goodness of God to Israel and his omniscience. But watching bad people experience the good life is too much. The Greek interpretation indicates that envy swept Asaph off his feet. His temper trips his heels and causes him to stumble. Have you ever tripped while strolling on an uneven sidewalk? Our little hometown has old, cracked sidewalks. My clumsiness has sent me head over heels more than once. Asaph's envy is a cracked sidewalk.

---

[54] Psalm 73: 1-20 (ESV).

And over what? The prosperity of the wicked. Asaph rages because they experience fewer troubles and calamities. In fact, they enjoy greater privileges. They live with pride thanks to their comfort and money but do not face punishment even in death. Not after they die, but in how they die. Their deaths are painless! The prideful experience earns no earthly (or eternal, according to Asaph) consequences for their big fat rich arrogance.

Note Asaph's internal and eternal struggle in verse 2:

> "I gloried in the goodness of God to Israel and His omniscience but almost tripped up."[55]

Look, this guy is not only suffering but is in anguish because people without a moral compass are not suffering. He wants them to feel the same pain and suffering others feel. This is not about reducing the stress and strife Asaph and the poor deal with but bringing the unjustly wealthy up to speed in the shame game. Weird.

This is human nature at work. How do we know someone is rich or poor if we do not know what the middle class looks like? This partially explains our need to compare. We talk social justice and economic equality, but Asaph wanted equal suffering.

When you think about it, Asaph held a unique perch between the poor and affluent. He certainly enjoyed an exalted position exposing him to the elite. Yet Asaph also identified with the struggling masses, which struggled with disease, poverty, hunger, and more. But Asaph was not focused on easing the suffering but sharing it.

Bottom line, trust in the absence of full understanding increases faith.

To his credit, Asaph identifies the existence of his weakness and thanks God for healing. Yet how did this mindset increase his personal pain? He assigned blame in lieu of seeking solutions to widespread suffering. This slowed Asaph's own healing and robbed him of the greatest blessing of all: the ability to forgive others.[56]

---

[55] Psalm 73: 2 (ESV).
[56] Walvoord, J.F., & Zuck, R.B. (2018).

Comparing does that. Asaph fretted over one question: "Why do these people have it so good? Or not so bad? How is that fair?" The comparison curse comes with one guarantee: you will reside safely outside God's will.

Pride is the source material of the curse. Whether comparison produces a sense of inferiority or superiority, pride is the source. This is true even if the final product is insecurity. The reality of comparison is you emerge believing you are either inferior or superior to your benchmark. Both thoughts are inaccurate and an abomination before God.

It actually leaves you angry toward God. Look at Asaph! He questioned why God would allow such a predicament. You speculate over God's will and ask why certain people are more blessed than us when the simple answer is they, too, question their meager blessings.

Some comparisons are a little out there. Peter is a prime example. Jesus frankly informs the disciple that his fate will be a martyr's death. Peter's choice to follow the Messiah carried that risk. Does Peter accept the prophecy or pray for a second opinion? Nope. He points at another person and asks if that fella receives the same fate. Martyrdom loves company, I suppose!

The comparison curse hammers home our misplaced criteria perhaps more than any other hurdle. It hits us where we live. We evaluate our existence based on whether other people have more or less. We ask the following questions:

1. Are they more comfortable and secure?
2. Are they more popular, do they have more friends, are they better liked?
3. Are their circumstances more positive?
4. Do they enjoy greater gratification, instant or otherwise?

The pursuit of these questions leaves us twisting in the wind.

Comparison leaves a void. We lack an identity in Christ, so we are without direction. In addition, the hope is not for God to bless us but for others to experience fewer blessings. We worry about how our existence measures up, but we are the ones destroying it by failing to count our blessings or even allowing God to bless us.

We truly should ask the following questions:

1. Why am I comfortable? What is my comfort zone?
2. Do I rely on the opinions of others to the point it forms

my self-worth?
3. Do circumstances drive my beliefs, or am I steadfast in the truth?
4. What brings me gratification? Is it instant or eternal?

Paul's words to the church of Corinth provide instruction:

"We do not dare to classify or compare ourselves with some who commend themselves. When they measure themselves by themselves and compare themselves with themselves, they are not wise."[57]

When is Paul a bad example? Never! Paul is responding to church members questioning his ability to keep long-held promises. Why? Paul apparently was unimpressive in person. He struggled with public speaking and self-promotion, at least according to his critics. Paul responds that he will never compare himself or his skills to the worldly skills honed by his critics. He is not competing with them in a popularity contest. Indeed, Paul argues his critics lack wisdom because they compete among themselves, and with Paul, in a game riddled with insignificance. They are "majoring in minors," as my grandmother used to say.

Do Paul's arguments hit a little too close to home? How can believers transform their thinking and attitudes? Here are some constructive approaches.

Identify with Christ and turn to him for understanding.

This is fairly straightforward and perhaps a bit too preachy for some. Let me put it another way: Our calling can only benefit from comparing our plight and circumstances to God's standards as opposed to the worldly standards or the standards of friends, family, and social network acquaintances. My attitude changed for the better when I decided to envision difficult times as God's preparation for something greater in my life. We all need to get our reps in, as one of my coaches loved to scream when we were running an endless serving of sprints.

A word from St. Peter: "But rejoice inasmuch as you participate in the sufferings of Christ, so that you may be overjoyed when his glory is revealed."[58]

Like Paul in Corinthians, Peter is speaking to new Christians. Accepting Jesus exposes you to persecution, so patiently deal with it, as

---

[57] 2 Cor 10: 12 (ESV).
[58] I Peter 4: 13 (ESV).

Peter directs them. He advises the flock to view persecution as normal, not as strange. Do not be surprised when difficult times emerge!

In addition, verse 14 indicates that Peter is focusing on lower levels of persecution: name-calling, slander, and so forth. Modern Christians experience that frequently, either in person or in the media. Yet we must persevere. You cannot be sad when the Spirit of God is resting on you. And verse 15 argues that we sometimes bring it on ourselves. I would prefer just suffering where the world is analyzing my intentional adherence to God's call as opposed to being part of the problem. We cannot suffer justly by committing evil.

Please note the kindness in Peter's approach. His trials and those of his audience are clearly at hand. This is just a quick reminder when Christ calls a man, he bids him come and die. Yet Peter argues we are in good company. Partaking in Christ's suffering is partaking in his glory.

Ask the right questions.

"Be still in the presence of the Lord and wait patiently for Him to act. Do not worry about wicked people who prosper or fret about their evil schemes." [59]

Unpleasant circumstances illustrate our need to build a stronger relationship with God by developing a greater understanding of that relationship. People naturally (due to human nature) respond to difficult times with questions. Indeed, we question God. Some prime examples:

- Why are you allowing this?
- What have I done wrong?

Why is so-and-so avoiding suffering? What is so great about him or her?

It is time to consider why so many inquiries of God start with why. Why not consider some "what" questions.

- What is my relationship with God?

This should lead to more probing questions such as:
- What are my priorities?
- What is my plan for spiritual growth? Do I have a plan for spiritual growth?

---

[59] Psalm 37: 7 (ESV).

- What are you teaching me, God?

Frankly, we should structure every day with these "whats" and make sure we evaluate God's answer. Do you have a curious mind? Curiosity comes in handy during trials. I also need to add they we should always ask how events shape us. My apologies for going off-script with a "how" question.

COMFORT OTHERS

"…who comforts us in all our troubles, so that we can comfort those in any trouble with the comfort we ourselves receive from God." "… When they are troubled, we will be able to give them the same comfort God has given us."[60]

Paul notes that God comforts us so we may comfort others. This is a personal message, as Paul suffered an affliction prior to penning this statement. Theologians grapple over the various trials or afflictions Paul mentions. That said, the prevailing assumption is that Paul is referring to persecution. Paul does not see this as an opportunity to vent but as a time to identify the practical benefits of suffering and persecution. And perhaps the biggest is how you can sincerely comfort other suffering believers because you share their pain.

The digital age created a comforting vacuum because few people are willing to express vulnerability thanks to the comparison trap. We must avoid looking feeble, helpless, or moving in the wrong direction. But I believe we are here to serve and care for each other. Has your calling transformed your vision? Perhaps the Holy Spirit corrected your vision so you can see the needs of this world and its inhabitants.

This remains possible only if you learn from your struggles and consider what God is teaching you. This is a subtle segue to the fourth approach.

Develop teachable spirits.

"Teach me your decrees, O Lord; I will keep them to the end."[61]

How do you learn something? This is (hopefully) my specialty. I teach students across the academic-skill spectrum. However, this

---

[60] 2 Cor. 1: 4 (ESV).
[61] Psalm 119: 33 (ESV).

approach (and book) focuses on attitude. My classes are filled with students looking for three hours credit and students who want an "A" to continue their march toward GPA domination. Sadly, neither group is truly learning but merely checking off a box on their worldly-criteria checklist. Yet my career also includes students probing the material with a "seek to understand" mindset. Apply this attitude to your daily walk and true learning is on the table. We will even outline an "eternal checklist" as a cheat sheet!

Bottom line, many Christians diligently pursue worldly gifts like career goals, money, possessions, or spouses. Apply that same zeal to knowing Christ better and it will crystallize your calling.

Be sensitized to suffering.

"If we are distressed, it is for your comfort and salvation; if we are comforted, it is for your comfort, which produces in you patient endurance of the same sufferings we suffer."[62]

Jesus made it clear that we will suffer (see John 15:20). Jesus and German pastor Dietrich Bonhoeffer suffered physical death. We could experience that or:

- Death of friendships
- Relationships
- Finances
- Employment

Because we:
- Confront hatred
- Shine the light of righteousness on sin

This means even when troubles weigh us down, it is for our comfort and salvation! For when we are comforted, we will comfort you. While this is similar to approach #3, it highlights that our pain sensitizes us to the pain of others. So the heartache this life brings us actually has a point.

People, events, and things build the foundation of our life. However, our life foundation can crack just like the foundation of your home, depending on how and where the builder constructed said dwelling. Moments like this leave us outside our worldly comfort zone.

---

[62] 2 Cor. 1: 6 (ESV).

However, chapter 7 explains why that can be a good thing and is even part of God's plan. Consider how living through God's eternal power transforms your calling.

CHAPTER 7
THE COMFORT ZONE

Trust in the LORD with all your heart
and lean not on your own understanding;
in all your ways submit to him,
and he will make your paths straight.
(Proverbs 3:5-6 ESV)

By wisdom the LORD laid the earth's foundations,
by understanding he set the heavens in place;
by his knowledge the watery depths were divided,
and the clouds let drop the dew.
My son, do not let wisdom and understanding out of your sight,
preserve sound judgment and discretion;
they will be life for you,
an ornament to grace your neck.
Then you will go on your way in safety,
and your foot will not stumble.
When you lie down, you will not be afraid;
when you lie down, your sleep will be sweet.
Have no fear of sudden disaster
or of the ruin that overtakes the wicked,
for the LORD will be at your side
and will keep your foot from being snared
(Proverbs 3:19-26, ESV).

God's wisdom is eternal. All believers pray for wisdom. Who among us would reject the wisdom of the ages? Solomon, the author of Proverbs, asked for wisdom when God gave the king an opportunity to choose anything. The world was on the table. Solomon selected the door with wisdom behind it. Why? Well, possessing the most powerful weapon or the largest bank account might prove futile without the ability to manage either resource prudently. Solomon also wanted to bless God as a ruler while not abusing everything at his disposal.[63]

My wife and I had a wonderful Bible study on the topic of wisdom. We explored how people accrued information, knowledge, and wisdom differently in the digital age. Earlier generations developed wisdom through the pursuit of information, as the process took time and was frankly arduous. Today, Google is your friend. Finding information is the least of your worries. The battle is determining what is real and what is garbage. What is true and what is fabricated. There is a decent chance none of the information finds the truth. This is why wisdom remains critical. Sifting through waves of data proves worthless absent a standard of truth guiding us.

So youngsters go after that godly wisdom and all is well. Sop it up on a biscuit! Your existence will trend in the right direction. Congrats!

How about we slow our roll just a tad? How did that wisdom thing work out for Solomon? Did the good king go to the wisdom well for every decision? We just might have some things to work out.

> The prophet Jeremiah can shed light on this.
> No one is like you, LORD;
> you are great,
> and your name is mighty in power.
> Who should not fear you,
> King of the nations?
> This is your due.
> Among all the wise leaders of the nations
> and in all their kingdoms,

---

[63] Walvoord, J.F., & Zuck, R.B. (2018). *The Bible Knowledge Commentary: Law*. Easy Sussex, England: David C. Cook.

there is no one like you.
They are all senseless and foolish;
they are taught by worthless wooden idols.
Hammered silver is brought from Tarshish
and gold from Uphaz.
What the craftsman and goldsmith have made
is then dressed in blue and purple—
all made by skilled workers.
But the LORD is the true God;
he is the living God, the eternal King.
When he is angry, the earth trembles;
the nations cannot endure his wrath.
"Tell them this: 'These gods, who did not make
the heavens and the earth, will perish from the
earth and from under the heavens.'"
But God made the earth by his power;
he founded the world by his wisdom
and stretched out the heavens by his
understanding.
When he thunders, the waters in the heavens
roar;
he makes clouds rise from the ends of the
earth.
He sends lightning with the rain
and brings out the wind from his storehouses.
Everyone is senseless and without knowledge;
every goldsmith is shamed by his idols.
The images he makes are a fraud;
they have no breath in them.
They are worthless, the objects of mockery;
when their judgment comes, they will perish.
He who is the Portion of Jacob is not like these,
for he is the Maker of all things,
including Israel, the people of his inheritance—
the LORD Almighty is his name.
—Jeremiah 10:6-16, ESV

Like Solomon, Jeremiah pursued and preached godly truth. God ultimately blessed the prophet for his faith. *Ultimately* is the keyword in that sentence. Jeremiah's ministry was hardly successful by worldly standards, his life anything but comfortable. This passage from Jeremiah chapter 10 explains the problem. God's wisdom is the truth. It carries eternal knowledge and extols the depth of the sacred. However, most folks never fully buy into God's plan over their own designs.[64]

People struggle with the complexity of God's wisdom. Indeed, few humans live by God's wisdom and most openly reject it in a hostile fashion. This includes even many believers, especially in the American church. The problem is God's wisdom typically runs counter to our own desires and dreams. We want to pursue command-number-one criteria in all its glory. We want to captain our own ship to achievement and accolades. Most of all, the wisdom of the ages challenges human nature, which hits us at our comfort level. We are living life on our own terms as opposed to God's terms. That is our comfort zone.

This chapter, in many ways, reflects the theme of this book. While fishing has never been what I would call a "comfortable" existence, Peter was familiar with this life. It supported his family. He was an expert in the field. So sacrifices were clearly made in following Jesus. And Jesus added comfort to their lives at least temporarily with the nets full of fish. They surrendered everything to the call.

Our question to ponder: what is God calling you to sacrifice? Which "creature comforts" sit on the chopping block? Confronting comfort remains a critical criterion in knowing whether you fully responded to God's calling. Too many pieces of evidence pointing to a comfortable existence probably means the answer is no.

Golf is not my game. So many friends swear by this expensive form of torture. One even remarked that he prayed to God that golf would be heaven. My response? "I could see golf in eternity."

My grandfather wanted me to be a golfer. He loved the game. He even gave me lessons. In fact, he spent hours working on my stance. The stance is obviously critical to golf, along with how you grip the clubs. Anyway, he finally had me positioned properly when asking a

---

[64] Walvoord, J.F., & Zuck, R.B. (2018). *The Bible Knowledge Commentary: Minor Prophets*. Easy Sussex, England: David C. Cook.

simple question:

Grandpa: Are you comfortable?

Me (lying!): Sure!

Grandpa: Then start over. If you are comfortable, you are doing it wrong!

Thus ended my first golf lesson.

Old Grandpa Bob was right. The effective golf stance (like the game itself) feels "unnatural," if that makes any sense. In fact, a round of golf removes you from the routine. The fast-paced multitasking gives way to slow concentrated deliberation. Success stems from slowing your mind and body, which proves very taxing. You walk away from the course mentally drained, but in a good way.

Golf reminds me of our Christian calling. This probably strikes you as odd, but frankly, if a Christian's walk is comfortable, then he or she is doing it all wrong. That completely misses God's model for following His call. Yet we pursue the comfort zone with everything we have.

I am no theologian. However, our divine purpose does not reside in the comfort zone. The rejection of eternal truth for worldly comfort remains a common thread through both testaments. Proverbs and Jeremiah are but two examples. The Israelites either fall prey to earthly pleasure or use God's truth for their own purpose. The problem is simple, though. Following biblical truth leads us to uncomfortable places, like the GPS sending me down remote country roads. The Holy Spirit sends us to scary locales where we cede control. And most people label us foolish for following this path and standing up for the truth.

Race and money are two big comfort zones. My research expertise includes urban development and theory, which has much to say about both topics. So examining urban development—which encompasses trends both ancient and modern—really takes us out of some deeply held American comfort zones. Few areas stoke fear and concern like otherness, especially in a socioeconomic context. This convinced me it was as good a start as any for piercing the comfort-zone bubble.

Chapter 7 attacks the human need for comfort and security. This book challenges the human need for comfort, security, and safety and analyzes our source of comfort and security. It remains fascinating how we cling to the familiar and comfortable. Seriously, the "comfort zone" is often a sad place. Like the Hebrew nation ready to hightail it back to Egypt at the first sign of desert-driven strife, we choose slavery over freedom!11

God wants us to flip our thinking when it comes to comfort and fear, as these are major biblical themes connecting all other themes. It is human nature to seek comfort or security. We believers pursue comfort in almost every aspect of our lives (career, church membership, community, politics, relationships, group affiliations). Yet God's plan is to pursue that which we fear. We must flip our thinking for that reason, but also because that which we fear is actually less harmful than that which we pursue.

COMFORTED BUT NOT COMFORTABLE

We have discussed suffering and persecution for a few chapters, so how about we go out on a high note?

The book of Romans provides an excellent template. Romans is Paul's unified vision of the gospel, which was passed orally from town to town at the time. Like a boxing or wrestling unification match, Paul is setting the record straight by outlining the real truth for all believers across the settled world. The missionary journeys exported the gospel to a diverse array of tribes, groups, and cultures. Each church developed its own truth, and some dealt with strict Pharisees still injecting their version of the law into the message of hope. Paul is communicating the one truth for his time and throughout history. He is also setting the scope of Christian doctrine.[65]

Imagine speaking to a class or group on the meaning of life as a Christian. How about a combative group of atheists? Now, what if you are called to defend the faith on television or, even worse, on Twitter or Instagram? That is the difference between the book of Romans and Paul's other letters. He is defending the Christian faith in front of the world at the epicenter of civilization at the time. The goal? Convince skeptics that Christ held the answer to life's questions while also explaining the truth to the Roman church members.

Paul is therefore defending the gospel and scriptural truth before

---

[65] Walvoord, J.F., & Zuck, R.B. (2018). *The Bible Knowledge Commentary: Acts & Epistles*. Easy Sussex, England: David C. Cook.

a diverse crowd at the epicenter of earthly existence. Does this shock us? The apostle accepted his role as defender of the faith in a spiritual war. I love history, especially wars. Two of my favorite college courses covered World War II and the Vietnam conflict. The courses examined decisions leaders made and the consequences. Professor and students alike sought a better understanding of why the winning side emerged victorious. Of course, we already knew which side "won," much like believers know who wins the eternal spiritual battle.

However, while Paul is concerned about being on the winning side, he also cares about the potential combat victims. What is their eternal destiny? Who will fight for their souls? Paul exhorts the audience that God forgives sins and is the door to not only a new life but also to a new eternal destination.

"For I am not ashamed of the gospel, for it is the power of God for salvation to everyone who believes, to the Jew first and also to the Greek. For in it the righteousness of God is revealed from faith to faith; as it is written, 'But the righteous man shall live by faith.'"[66]

Paul is speaking to non-believers but also to members of the flock stuck in the law. The law can do many things—teach, guide, explain God to us, but it cannot energize our flesh. It gives us a standard but not the power to live in a manner that pleases God. The law of the Spirit is the only law that overcomes the law of death and sin.[67]

That is the odd comfort-zone fact. Christians equate the comfort zone with the community of believers or the church. We all believe the same thing, right? However, that is hardly the case. Also, we presume our fellow flock friends are living the perfect lives God gave them. But are those lives truly perfect?

How does the church envision membership and commitment? The American faithful expect their local flock to provide comfort and fellowship. This is fine to a certain extent and includes several aspects of God's plan. However, the mindset for worship is consumption-oriented. Are we missing the point? Is God's house meant to be a hotel or resort where perfect people meet to hone their perfections, or is it a hospital for hurt souls seeking comfort that only our heavenly savior

---

[66] Romans 1: 16-17 (ESV).
[67] Walvoord, J.F., & Zuck, R.B. (2018).

can provide? Which metaphor best describes your experience?

LESSONS FROM BOTH MOVEMENTS

Obviously, doing the right thing is hard when the wrong thing is profitable. Or comfortable. You will encounter massive resistance depending on whose toes you may step on in your quest. The deep reveal from this illustration is that following God means rejecting the world at some level.

Additionally, God's plan for our lives (and this world) prioritizes pursuing eternal significance as opposed to earthly transformation. And this really hits at the heart of the problem. The social gospel called for a man-made deliverance that ignored the providential hand of God. This may be the worst characteristic of a movement built on strange theology.

Jeremiah could attest to all of this. His walk checked all the criteria boxes. Perhaps he never quite assumed an exalted worldly position as he sacrificed his plans before they even got started. Jeremiah's walk is unique in that he never truly tasted worldly success or struggled with popularity.

Jeremiah was extremely unpopular and alone. As in really disliked by many. This was his cross to bear. Popularity seems so lightweight compared to the other-world criteria. However, is it fair to say people crave fame? I think a quick look at social media and reality TV answers that question. We love being recognized. Some people love it so much they pursue "eyeballs at all costs" or recognition for the wrong reasons.

In addition, God made us for fellowship, so even having friends and family who love you and offer trusting, honest relationships is critical. We need believers to confide in and share our concerns and challenges. God has blessed me with several accountability groups throughout my adult life. I find it hard to fully measure the value of having people you trust listen to raw, unfiltered you.

Jeremiah missed all of that, as far as we know. Why? God's plan. Jeremiah's prophetic message was so unpopular it incited loathing. We need to work through the criteria for our Jeremiah evaluation.

Success

Scripture indicates Jeremiah lead two people to the Lord over the course of his ministry. His destiny at birth was entering the pastoral ministry, but God had other plans. Therefore, Jeremiah's ministerial "record of achievement" is sparse at best.

Circumstances

Jeremiah endured the worst circumstances, which is saying something. He lived through Judah's descent into exile and captivity. His providential timing was the worst! Additionally, this occurred during a wave of pagan idol worship, which leads us to our next criterion.

Popularity

Both leadership and the people hated Jeremiah because he was an honest prophet, merely echoing God's message. To be fair, "Yes, you are going to lose, and yes, it is your fault!" is hardly an effective campaign slogan. Do you know what a consultant does? A good consultant knows his or her stuff but also clearly identifies the steps for improvement. For example, say you own a small business hemorrhaging cash. You hire a consultant to explain why the business is losing money and how to reverse the trend via an open, frank conversation.

The kings never hired good consultants as prophets. They hired "yes men" who parroted their message to the people. The message was that all is well and God will protect us. Jeremiah refused to be a "yes man," and we speak of him in reverence for that very reason. Yet Jeremiah's reception was far colder at the time.

Jeremiah criticized leadership. And he suffered for it. God's prophet endured prison and death threats and plots against his life, and he ended up in the bottom of a cistern. Everyone, including religious leaders, governing leaders, and the people, rejected his message because it did not fit their agenda. Jeremiah failed to support their actions, so it was concluded that he could never speak for God

Instant Gratification

Instant gratification? Did Jeremiah ever experience gratification of any sort? He endured years of ridicule and angst followed by captivity, which eventually lasted for centuries. Frankly, most folks would polish the resume.

Again, the Hebrews worshiped idols and adhered to the practice of making their own gods out of available materials such as stones, glass, and wood. This included fertility gods and worshiping at fertility poles with prostitutes. Therefore, their allegiance to the one true God was nonexistent.

However, do you know what really irked God (and Jeremiah by extension)? God's people chased idolatry based on what was "working" at the moment. One of God's (and Jeremiah's) biggest frustrations was not only did the Hebrews worship idols but they were also not consistent. At least the pagans stuck with it in good times and bad.

Does the Hebrew mindset sound familiar? Do believers today opt for worldly actions either by design, superstition, or by what seems to yield to their desires? It happens frequently without concern for God's plan.

JEREMIAH'S LEGACY

My employer's mission is to build Christian leaders for future generations and eternity. Our motto is taken from Jeremiah 29:11. The prophets, both major and minor, walked similar paths paved with consistent messages. God's people had failed Him, and thus, an eternal covenant lay broken but (and biblical buts are critical) God still loved them and cared for them. This meant He would restore broken covenants on His timetable.

Jeremiah communicated that message and experienced the pain and suffering from captors as well as his people. Jeremiah's legacy is secure and eternal, but those realizations did not occur during his time on earth. Granted, his dire predictions and warnings proved correct, which offered a small consolation.

Yet Jeremiah adhered to God's call regardless of the earthly outcome because he believed in the eternal outcome. His legacy provides perhaps the most apt example of this book's thesis: align your life with God's criteria.

What about us? How does our commitment compare to Jeremiah's sacrifice? And what would that sacrifice look like in our lives? It could mean a complete 180-degree shift where you move on from the familiar. Quit your job? Maybe. It could also mean reorienting your approach to work and calling. The next chapter discusses providential decision-making.

CHAPTER 8
INSTANT GRATIFICATION

"That tree you rested under. Someone planted it a long time ago."
—Warren Buffett, legendary investor[68]

The modern world has rid us of that stifling notion called patience. We can get most anything immediately, so why wait? Why play the long game? Tomorrow is not promised to us so enjoy today and order from Amazon!

Do you binge-watch TV shows? What a 2022 question! My youthful viewing habits mandated the weekly delay, as I sat in school wondering where the favorite shows were heading next week! Well, that is not a problem in the streaming world, save a few exceptions. Each audience member controls his or her plot-consumption fate.

Frankly, this makes for a wonderful psychological experiment. Psychological researchers have devoted hours and years (along with millions in grant dollars) studying the driving impulse of instant gratification. One of the earliest examples involved marshmallows, of all things. Professors and researchers would leave preschool children in a room with one solitary marshmallow per child and the promise of a second pillowy snack if the child waited for the adult to return before eating marshmallow number one. The researcher then waited fifteen minutes before returning to the room to see if the first marshmallow remained on the table. Bottom line, some kids got a

---

[68] Friedman, Zack. *Here Are 10 Genius Quotes From Warren Buffett.* Forbes.com. October 4, 2018. *https://www.forbes.com/sites/zackfriedman/2018/10/04/warren-buffett-best-quotes/?sh=4e9e3f9f4261*

second marshmallow while most were one and done.[69]

The researchers were merely getting started. They held additional studies of the same children and found that those children who patiently waited for the double dip lived better lives on a range of measures such as SAT scores and obesity levels. Patience is indeed a virtue, as my mother was always quick to remind me. So just wait and good things happen, right? Not always. This lesson ignores the unpredictable nature of life. Patience is built on a pillar of trust in people, providence, and fate.[70] Consider the barriers to receiving a second marshmallow. The kiddoes faced:

1. The uncertain period of time. We see fifteen minutes, but the pursuit of dreams, goals, or even plans can run for days, months, and years with no clear evidence a solution is over the horizon.
2. The mirage. A brief victory indicates the end is near, but the battle has only begun.
3. A marshmallow in hand. Why worry about the second snack when I already have a perfectly tasty treat composed of sugar and air?

Indeed, being patient is a challenge even when you know the end is near and how long it will take. Circling back to the binge-watching illustration, my wife and I have very different binging approaches. She takes the instant-gratification approach, consuming several episodes or even seasons in one sitting. In contrast, I play the long game to savor what I am watching. Now, watching the same show remains a stakes-filled endeavor, with both parties compromising on the viewing pace. Subject matter is a big player here as well. I am more amenable to consuming comedies/sitcoms, but tension-building dramas (or, heaven forbid, romcoms!) require a break. In addition, length factors in, as twenty minutes goes down much smoother than a fifty-minute slog.

And now, back to generations accustomed to instant delivery with everything at our fingertips.

The world encourages instant gratification. Our economy builds on immediate, conspicuous consumption. The less time we spend

---

[69] *https://jamesclear.com/delayed-gratification*
[70] Working on a different P word.

considering our decisions or actions, the better. Same with how we interpret the world around us and God's plan for it. Excess information has a way of drawing our attention away from eternal priorities.

A small lesson from my teaching. The course material includes the media among the end-of-semester topics. The section commences by contrasting "old media" versus "new media" approaches. Have you ever watched an old news broadcast or read a newspaper? I am speaking to the younger readers here as most of my fellow "seasoned" consumers presumably grew up on the model. The news cycle utilized a deliberative pace so reporters or broadcasters could peel away the layers of a story like an onion until the full truth emerged. The process had its negatives. Newsgathering and delivery were hardly efficient back in the day, with tons of ink wasted to deliver stale information. However, the old-media approach did foster journalistic accuracy and depth. Those reigned as the old-school priorities.

Today, new media occur at a more rapid pace. The new paradigm typically condenses the news cycle into a matter of seconds. We learn of the latest election/disaster/controversy/Kardashian party minutes after the happening occurs, even if details are sketchy. This only pokes at what the gatekeepers designate as newsworthy. The old media focused on critical events, while twenty-four-hour networks need content to fill valuable broadcast real estate. Being first, fast, and filler reign as the new priorities.

Moreover, those dastardly millennial/Generation Z digital natives operate in this instant gratification chamber of fun/horrors. Social media devices spit out instant information, which everyone assumes to be true given the sources. And that is merely the accrual of news, whether it be local, national, or global. The younger generations develop community via social devices, which replace the old media, such as newspapers, but also other institutions such as churches. Social networking stresses instant connection and instant community, which cuts out the hard, grueling part of getting to know people and patiently working together through our personal eccentricities.

Yet I must avoid pointing the finger at the younger folks, and not merely because that makes me look old. Frankly, most everyone I know or encounter experienced the appreciation for delayed gratification thanks to social networks. Gone is the acknowledgement of what a person or community can accomplish by merely waiting.

Our model Peter knew very little instant gratification. He was a fisherman after all, and any angler, whether professional or recreational, will tell you the fish sometimes do not cooperate. Jesus probably appreciated this learned patience. Of course, Peter's legacy and our understanding of his ministry include several impatient moments. For example, he exclaims to Jesus that all the disciples have given up everything to follow Him after the meeting with the rich young ruler.[71] Jesus basically responds that it will all be worth it. Eventually.

Peter "eventually" comes around to this long-term mindset. The letters he penned toward the end of his life addressed the young churches fraught with frustration (and fear thanks to Nero's organized persecution) over Jesus's delayed second coming. Peter preached patience:

"But do not overlook this one fact, beloved, that with the Lord one day is as a thousand years, and a thousand years as one day. The Lord is not slow to fulfill his promise as some count slowness, but is patient toward you, not wishing that any should perish, but that all should reach repentance."[72]

The student clearly listened to his teacher.

Doug is a good friend and attorney. We have a standing monthly lunch to mostly catch up on life and chat over what is working in our world and what needs work. Doug is a talker with much to say, yet he is saying something as opposed to just making noise. That said, he always seems to save the juicy stuff for the parking lot after lunch is over and I need to get back to the office. These nuggets are morsels of substance and take a while to savor and fully digest. This is a fancy way of saying that yes, Doug tells entertaining stories and provides valuable information. But he clearly adheres to the "old media" conversation, if you catch my drift.

And Doug is very consistent. He utilized a recent post-lunch seminar to regale me with stock market talk. A very large investment paid off in a big way as Doug had just sold his shares a few weeks prior to our lunch. The hook of the story? Doug made that significant

---

[71] Matthew 19:16-30 (ESV).
[72] Matt: 19: 16-30 (ESV).

investment in 2001 and held the shares for almost 20 years! "I just understood the markets and knew that sector was ripe for growth. I bought it and watched it appreciate."

See what merely waiting can accomplish?

Why do experts tell workers to start planning (and funding) retirement as soon as possible? Because compounding is the key to investing. My oldest son recently asked me to help him with an economics project. I was beside myself with joy. He let me pick the topic from a batch of econ nuggets such as Federal Reserve requirements, inflation, and employment. My choice? The rule of 72.

The rule is simple. Divide 72 by the return on investment (ROI) and that is how long it takes your money to double.[73] For example, let's say you have a $1,000 investment paying 8 percent. Dividing 72 by 8 equals nine. So you will have $2,000 in nine years if you just leave it alone.

Here is a hypothetical situation. Pretend I am in a "giving cycle" lasting one month. Pretend I double the "donation" every day, so your day two bounty is twice the amount of day 1, and day 3 doubles day 2. Not too shabby!

One more detail: your day 1 payoff is a penny. Yes, $.01. A copper Abe.

So how much do you have after thirty days? You have a whopping .01 after day 1, .03 after day 2, and .07 after day 3. By the end of week 1, you are sitting on a $1.96 cumulative. But how about after thirty days? $10,596,434. Yes, I owe you over $10 million!

Such is the power of compounding. It fuels the investing engine. Economists consider compound investing a fiscal miracle. Do you want a fiscal miracle in your life? Of course, you do! Remember our good friend Jim from chapter 4? The one with the ERA? Consider how much Jim and other workers invest during their careers. He set a percentage of his income monthly or bimonthly for more than forty years. This is why you start early. Jim almost assuredly made less income during his early days, but those formative investments probably compounded or doubled at least four to five times for a 500 percent return!

---

[73] Kenton, Will. *Rule of 72*. Investopedia.com. March 10, 2021. *https://www.investopedia.com/terms/r/ruleof72.asp*

My friend Doug possesses faith in himself and his investing ability. His faith surmounted the urges to sell. Doug knew what he was doing. "I know how the stock market works." Delayed gratification requires such faith, as most people live on the instant-gratification trail and lack faith. Yet the rule of 72 rejects instant gratification.

Delayed gratification remains a proven tool for success. It should be a big part of your career plan. However, our calling demands eternal gratification. Eternal gratification requires more than faith in ourselves. It requires faith in God.

The biblical narrative flows with examples of eternal gratification. Indeed, waiting is a major scriptural theme. So many people waited on God to transform their lives, but I would like to discuss a big name in particular. Abraham. Why Abraham?

Three reasons actually:

1. We never give Abraham his full due. This is not a critical theological truth, but it just bugs me.

    My memory might be flagging a bit, but Sunday school for children seems to jump from Eden to Babel, followed by Noah and the flood, which took us to Moses. Did the teachers mention Abraham? Did we color Abraham-themed pages? That probably happened, but the memories fail to stick. This is odd, as Abraham's story has drama, but Genesis is packed with it, so perhaps we gloss over his part. At least the young me did.

2. He is a critical "covenant cog," which means his testimony is directly woven into God's eternal plan.

    Yes, this is heavy theological stuff we will try to unpack. What is a covenant? People often say it is a type of contract, which is not entirely accurate. A covenant is a morally informed agreement or pact based upon voluntary consent, established by mutual oaths, or promises involving or witnessed by some transcendent higher authority, between peoples or parties having independent status. Every covenant involves consenting (in both senses of thinking together and agreeing) and promising. Most are meant to be of unlimited duration, if not perpetual.

    Covenants can bind any number of partners for a variety of

purposes, but in their essence, they are political in that their bonds are used principally to establish bodies political and social. We see in Genesis 12 how God uses the Abrahamic covenant to renew his original creation purposes locally after confusing human speech and scattering the people worldwide. In this covenant, God promises that the Redeemer will come through Abraham's descendants in the nation of Israel.

Bottom line, in this covenant, Abraham's relationship with God becomes the basis for all other covenants. And covenants, while legal, really are committed relationships, and the covenant solidifies that commitment and explains the purposes of the relationship. So yes, Abe and the covenant are crucial, but this is really about the relationship between God and a faithful follower.[74]

3. Abraham's testimony clearly illustrated gratification, both delayed and eternal.

   In fact, his Kingdom contribution remains perhaps the truest example of eternal gratification. Yet when God approached Abraham with the covenant proposal, Abraham was not in a waiting mode desperately seeking God's favor. And he still accepted the covenant and thus surrendered his life to the calling. Why is Abraham connected to our little project? God chose him, and he went even though he was seventy-five and comfortable. Abraham believed and acted on faith. Did God's promise include worldly benefits? Yes, that was part of the deal, but the Creator urged Abraham to fix his eyes on bigger goals. Abraham's faith is an active faith where he believes God will do as promised and blessings ensue, although the biggest come after he left this life.[75]

   Abraham's story should encourage each of us. He is seventy, and we have heard little about him. This is kind of exciting and hopeful to me because Abraham is like us. Scripture

---

[74] Genesis 12:1 (ESV).
[75] Hebrews 11:8-10, (ESV).

details the lives of great warriors, kings, brilliant writers, and scholars. Abraham was none of these. Was he perfect? Negative. We read several references to big mistakes where he thought, *I will help God out here.* Have you ever done that? I think this is God's will, but it is impossible to know, so how about we come up with a plan? When you are afraid to dive in, remember you have a lifeguard.

THE WISDOM OF LONG-TERM PLANNING

Paul's life exhorts us to take the same attitude with our eternal purpose. Jim seeks to live this out and leave an eternal legacy. Our purpose, in a way, plays out like the rule of 72. Our career and work can yield compounding blessings like Paul's if we take his lesson and Jim's attitude to heart.

God can use you to produce compounding blessings if only you buck the status quo to max out your calling like Paul. Because your life can have a compounding impact on the Kingdom if you take Paul's lesson to heart. Clearly, his ERA can yield compounding blessings.

How can your calling yield compounding blessings? What are your skills and calling elements? What must change in these areas of your character? What is your holy capital? My purpose in writing this book is to help you address and hopefully answer these questions.

Bottom line, what does an eternal investment look like? How does it change your career? Your life? How does it affect where you work and how you spend your time? Investing in one's Christian life is risky. Are you willing to accept the risks necessary for compounding blessings? What changes must you accept as non-negotiable?

Bottom line, commit to acting upon the prescribed plan! This book will achieve success if it can play a small role in moving believers from a passive, consumption-driven church experience built on comfort to active, mission-driven believers.

In fact, that ultimately is the focus of this book. The five criteria chapters highlighted worldly motivations blocking us from eternal significance. We spent these pages examining "people priorities," including characteristics and emotions yielding temporal happiness.

Dreams and delusions alike drive our plans for world domination or perhaps at least worldly recognition. While we would love to identify positive sources for our motives, shame and its nasty twin pride typically push us forward as our past continues to haunt us. Shame ensnares us in the comparison trap where we cannot escape fretting over why God blesses other people, even friends and family, more than us. While the comparison trap is deadly, the comfort zone proves to be equally perilous. We strive for security and seek distance between danger and ourselves, but is that our calling? Finally, we want all these things and none of the bad things instantly, along with the answers to any questions keeping us up at night.

This is our mindset. Yet the five chapters also examined the mindset of scriptural heroes who sacrificed everything or at least possessed a willingness to sacrifice everything for the Kingdom. These Kingdom builders followed God's eternal blueprint in lieu of their own design. Conversely, we remain empire strivers looking to leave our mark while enjoying the fruit of our labor and the benefits of revered worldly adulation.

However, Jim is a modern-day Kingdom builder sacrificing the fruits of his career labors for eternal blessings. He and his wife will not experience those blessings in this life, and they are good with that. In fact, my guess is they are fine with leaving all the accolades of their giving to others who need it. Yes, Jim did tell me about their decision, but it seemed more in explanatory mode than a humble brag one. A modest life yielding a vast and major impact.

We have come to a pivot much like the Abrahamic covenant. Where do we go from here? The pivot is from a descriptive mode to prescriptive. Our readings explained what an empire striver looks like and how they think contrasted with the Kingdom builder mindset. We devote the final chapters describing both models and how to pivot to eternal goals. This begins with chapter 9 explaining the consequences of the empire mindset and what it looks like with our Savior's biggest earthly enemies serving as the model.

CHAPTER 9
CONSEQUENCES— WHAT CAN GO WRONG?

Okay, we dissected each criterion thoroughly. Five chapters should be enough for anyone! You are now privy to the mirror images for each pair. So where does that leave us? Well, chapter 8 indicated we now have a decision to make. This leaves us at an eternal crossroads. Like all decisions, either direction carries consequences. Moreover, these consequences are eternal.

Standing at the crossroads indicates change will happen. We are speaking of internal change, but what if we looked at a macro example? How does change occur in communities or societies?

One of the more basic answers is contact or proximity. A convergence of diverse societies or communities dwelling in close proximity or contact with each other produces rapid change. Intercultural contact and communication occur naturally (if not awkwardly), which hopefully yields mutual understanding.

How does contact occur? The usual suspects are trade and war. This is a (light) economic work, so the focus is on trade. The process mimics city development: goods and people connected by transportation. The ancients had bridges and seafaring vessels delivering people and products. Trade linked the early world and altered cultures.[76]

But which communities experienced the deepest and most rapid change? Those positioned at the crossroads. An accepted social-change axiom is growing populations increase the likelihood of social change, but communities existing at the crossroads are even more likely to experience seismic cultural shifts. Economists would label world trade centers as crossroads, but change was not just a currency. Trade brought people, communities, and cultures together, which ushered in historic changes.

The early church experienced this, understood it, and ultimately

---

[76] *http://www.sociologyguide.com/social-change/factors-of-change.php*

embraced it as God's plan. The outreach and transformation that persecution set in motion reached every outpost of the Roman Empire, particularly cosmopolitan trade centers where evangelism became a chief export. God's providence and guiding hand created the early church at the crossroads of the world. A body of believers was connected by faith yet marked by their own distinctives. Do we think this happened by chance or by a divine, providential blueprint?[77]

Placing the church at the crossroads of civilization launched the early global church. That said, this author believes economic development has launched this process once again. Our world is at a major crossroads thanks to globalization! Indeed, the cover art illustrates a reality: the global map is a giant crossroads intersecting the whole of humanity, with lives brought together digitally and geographically.

This chapter deals with escaping our personal inertia to experience change. However, this involves consequences in either direction.

Say you chose number one. How bad can it be? After all, Jesus blessed the disciples (and non-disciples) in a material sense. How does this look? What are some on-point biblical examples?

NEGATIVE EXAMPLE: THE PHARISEES

I would start with the Pharisees, a constant thorn in Peter's side, especially in his efforts to establish and build the early church. Most readers identify Pharisees as the group driving the crucifixion of Jesus. That would be correct. However, I endeavor to highlight why they pushed for that result. Which personal interests motivated their attack of Jesus and the movement he spawned?

And now, a few disclaimers:
- I am not calling anyone a Pharisee!
- I also am not saying Pharisees are solely responsible for the crucifixion.
- I also am not saying that pursuing success in a career or any other aspect of life makes you a Pharisee.
- This is merely an illustration!

---

[77] Book of Acts (ESV).

Who were the Pharisees? Or better yet, what were the Pharisees? My plan is to tread through this analysis carefully. Again, this book sheds light on my fleshly weaknesses. This illustration simply shines a light on the motivations driving the Pharisaic response to Jesus's message.
1. The sect members possessed a deep reservoir of worldly power and authority.
2. They craved control in order to preserve their worldly authority and power source.
3. The Pharisees also profited from Scripture and the law, which also motivated their desire to force the people to adhere to their legal interpretation.
4. Again, the members benefitted from the arrangement, which led to their "whoring out the gospel" in my analysis.[78]

And therein lies the Pharisaic connection to our thesis. Group members possessed a stake in the status quo. How does the narrative impact our understanding of God's calling in our lives? This is what command-number-one believers do. This historical review of their actions and motivations helps us identify how we fall prey to preserving our reservoir of worldly power and profit from our faith in pursuit of the wrong criteria.

Who or what were the Pharisees? Some sources label them a political party, while others call it a religious group. Which is correct? Both labels are accurate, as it turns out.

Given Israel's theocratic structure, religious leaders carried political authority as well as theological heft.

Specifically, the Pharisees were the most popular Great Sanhedrin faction. The Great Sanhedrin functioned as a supreme court/senate hybrid carrying out legal and political edicts. The president during the period of the crucifixion was Gamaliel. Gamaliel led the Pharisees and is perhaps most famous today for mentoring noted scribe Saul, who eventually became the apostle, Paul.[79]

Yet Paul and Gamaliel were hardly the only famous Pharisees of

---

[78] Ancient Jewish History: Pharisees, Sadducees & Essenes. Jewish Virtual Library. *https://www.jewishvirtuallibrary.org/pharisees-sadducees-and-essenes*
[79] Jewish Virtual Library.

the day. The group actually broke into two factions, similar to modern-day political parties facing internal dissension over accepted dogma or policy purity. A rabbi named Shammai founded the ultra-conservative/orthodox sect. Shammai hated non-Jews and built the brotherhood upon enforcing rules, commandments, and Hebrew superiority. Modern Christians tend to equate such Pharisaic authority with merely enforcing God's law, but Shammai's goals were driving a wedge between Jews and Gentiles. Indeed, he penned eighteen edicts designed to accomplish that objective.

The rabbi Hillel led the "competing" faction by stressing people over principles. The school of Hillel adhered to the same principles as Shammai but prayed that the people would see the error of their ways. This faction also welcomed Gentile converts. Hillel was Gamaliel's grandfather, so his legacy influenced Paul even though Paul joined the Shammai school in stoning heretics challenging their law.[80]

While this description sounds troubling, we have yet to hammer home what made the Pharisees truly reprehensible. Perhaps the gospels of Matthew and Luke can shine a light on their true nature.

Both disciples listed the "woes of the Pharisees," although Matthew penned two more woes than did Luke. Either way, both lists highlighted the hypocrisy and internal rot characterizing the group. The woes flowed from the group's self-serving enforcement of the law. Additionally, the sect members practiced the highest forms of hypocrisy and self-righteousness, which happens when someone is more devoted to rules and religions than God. And the rot extended over all of Israel as Pharisees enjoyed enormous power and control. They even profited from their power over the law.

This explains their loathing of Jesus. His ministry and following diluted their power. The Pharisees derived authority from controlling the law and the synagogues. Jesus rejected the entire Pharisaic worldview by arguing they abused Scripture and the law for their own gain. This shed a light on their true motives. The Pharisees loved money. This was at least partially a theological position built on the belief that poverty was God's punishment for a sinful life. Yet the sect leveraged theological beliefs for monetary reward. Jesus screamed that the core was rotten,

---

[80] Ibid.

which made him dangerous.[81]

However, something or someone is dangerous because they are a threat to that which has value. Burglars serve as a threat to possessions and murderers, a threat to life. Jesus was a threat because he fought for change, which forced the sect to fight for what members "rightfully" earned, including worldly security, comfort, and status.

The group's influence (and interference) hardly waned during the early church era. Some Pharisees who converted did not want gentiles, while others wanted gentiles to follow the law. The Council of Nicene dealt with these arguments, which compromised the global gospel explosion and Paul's missionary journeys. Indeed, the apostle constantly expressed frustration over his fellow brethren even though he remained a Pharisee until the end.[82]

How does an ancient sect responsible for crucifying Jesus connect with our lives? The gospels pile it on when criticizing the Pharisees. They are just the worst! That said, we tend to take the labels *hypocrisy* and *legalistic* at face value without probing below the surface. This does not question the veracity of the gospels. Indeed, my goal is digging deeper. For example, our thesis requires me to ponder why the Pharisees pursued their beliefs and specific courses of action. In addition, how did they engage in hypocrisy, what are the consequences, and how does that shine a light on our motives?

First, how do the Pharisees measure in our analysis? Well, they craved control over the Law, synagogue, and people. They felt the shame of the existing circumstances as pride blinded them to their abusing the truth. What about the comparison trap? The sect members fought other groups, such as the Sadducees. They possessed comfort by perpetuating their own truth and living in an echo chamber. They ignored pain and needs outside the synagogue. Finally, the Pharisees enjoyed the instant gratification that earthly control, power, and respect promise at least temporarily.[83]

The charges facing the Pharisees were accurate, but why did the sect crave control? Shammai founded the Pharisees as a "law enforcer"

---

[81] Sproul, R.C. *Why Did the Pharisees Hate Jesus So Much?*
[82] Walvoord, J.F., & Zuck, R.B. (2018). *The Bible Knowledge Commentary: Acts*. Easy Sussex, England: David C. Cook.
[83] Walvoord, J.F., & Zuck, R.B. (2018).

tasked with keeping the nation in line to avoid God's wrath and the ensuing captivity.[84] The group feared domination by another culture and sought to preserve autonomy by forcing Israelites to adhere to God's law. What is wrong with that? Well, the law cannot save us, as Paul frequently reminded us in the epistles. This assumes we possess control over our eternal fate. Additionally, the "salvation" Pharisees craved was worldly and in this life. They were not pursuing eternal blessings, merely temporal. Still, we can at least sympathize with the initial motives. How would patriotic Americans respond to such a threat?

However, the group whored out God's law for their own benefit. Early schools wove their hatred of gentiles and Jews sympathetic to the gentile plight into the list of excluded activities and practices. Of course, members often ignored their own laws, hence the hypocrisy accusations. They also insisted that the law exalted the wealthy while punishing the poor. Most critically, the sect leveraged the sacred for financial gain. These acts merely reinforced earthly authority and control.

Bottom line, the Pharisees serve as a cautionary tale because they prioritized their earthly reputation over true character. They focus squarely on external outcomes as opposed to internal motives. The group failed to consider the eternal possibilities flowing from everything God provided them. The concern over consolidating earthly power and reward clouded their judgment and eternal vision.

And therein lies our connection. What motives drive you? Which criteria best describe your priorities? Have you considered the eternal consequences of your actions and decisions? Do you act according to eternal truth or with a focus on consolidating your worldly authority and assets, i.e., the command-number-one approach to life.

Does the command-number-one life make you or me a Pharisee? Well, not fully, one hundred percent Pharisees. The sect members were intentional with their actions. They committed atrocities in the name of God and His Law while really enriching themselves materially and enhancing the group's power. Our shortcomings tend to fall under the sins of omission category. Or ignorance, perhaps. We struggle with truly realizing our eternal impact. Frankly, that is not an excuse, nor does it make sense to grade sin levels. That said, maybe we can lean on the

---

[84] Jewish Virtual Library.

criminal justice system. Criminal acts are merely one side of the penal code. A perpetrator's brain is also critical. Intentional crimes carry much heavier penalties than negligent acts. Also, sometimes the consequences go worse than planned, such as a bank robbery that results in murder. The robbers should have predicted someone might get hurt, but since the death was not "premeditated," they could face a lower offense. The consequences of their actions are worse than their motives.

Sadly, this is where we are at this point. This chapter is about consequences, and the results of our motives and actions look remarkably similar to the Pharisees, even though their business model included persecution. The sect eventually pursued preserving and expanding their control and authority in this life by altering the sacred for their own purposes. While the Pharisees were certainly not solely responsible for the crucifixion, their role was significant.[85] Interestingly, their role of gospel blockage increased after the cross. The Pharisees eventually assumed secular dominance over Jerusalem after emerging victorious from the battle of various Sanhedrin factions. This solidified their law and obedience-driven policies until the temple fell in 70 AD. In addition, this summary of atrocities would be incomplete without describing the Pharisees who eventually joined the Christian movement yet could not abandon their legalistic ways, potentially stifling the gentile missionary effort. Their craven motives scarred the beauty of God's creation with their filth-ridden earthly agenda.[86]

So how do the consequences of our actions compare to those consequences? After all, we did not intend to compromise God's plan. Right? Any consequences are unintentional. Nevertheless, here is the thing about unintended consequences: they often wreak as much or more damage as the planned counterparts. Unintended consequences are so potentially awful that public policy analysts stress over the unintended consequences of laws. Free-market economics is essentially the study of unintended consequences. For example, raising the minimum wage should put more money in the pockets of low-income workers,

---

[85] The Sadducees played a larger role in the trial and punishment of Jesus. Indeed, much of the deceit and violence lay at their feet. Most of the acts of manipulation and deception leading to the cross that you read in the gospels were from this sect.
[86] Walvoord, J.F., & Zuck, R.B. (2018).

but the new law could also increase unemployment, as firms cannot afford to keep all their employees. Congress banned price increases of staple products in the 1970s to battle inflation, which only reduced the available supply of said staples, which increased demand and the cost of living as well. What are the unintended consequences of following command number one? My explanation focuses on one cultural area.

Art. Specifically the theft of rare art. How does art explain eternal consequences? Recently, art and art theft started emerging as a growing fascination of mine. This will never replace sharks, but still interesting stuff. A documentary covering a major 1990 theft at the Gardner Museum in Boston got me rolling. Two thieves sporting Boston police gear entered the poorly guarded museum and made off with thirteen precious items valued at $80 million. The haul included Rembrandt's haunting *Jesus and the Storm on the Sea of Galilee,* created in 1633.[87] The work echoes characteristics I especially appreciate about art or at least certain works of art. Of course, Rembrandt chose a sacred subject, which is wonderful, but he crafted an action shot. The image is mid-story which is great. It also captures the response of each disciple and Jesus and even looks dynamic as opposed to frozen in time. Wonderful piece, which captures a wonderful subject.

Now it is gone, and the world will most likely never see the original again. Rembrandt created a masterpiece for generations to enjoy, yet someone stole that opportunity.

My question (as always) is why? You knew I would ask this question. Why do people steal art? The obvious answer is not so obvious, actually. "Money" is the obvious answer, and that is a factor. However, profiting from stolen art requires finding a buyer without raising suspicion. I often hear the verb "fencing," as in "he was caught fencing stolen goods," but fencing a piece everyone is looking for seems like more trouble than it is worth.

A little research went a long way toward answering the "why," as it turned out. The art heist seems like a high-tone, erudite game played by sophisticated rapscallions looking to possess work that speaks to their heart or utilize tony, old-money connections to move the piece for rich

---

[87] Barnicle, C (Director), Barnicle, N (Producer). (2021). *This is a Robbery.* Netflix streaming series. Boston: Barnicle Brother Production; Tribeca Productions. Distributed by Netflix

connections. Indeed, art heist movies and books regale us with bored millionaires and billionaires needing to capture the thrill of the chase.

We love books and movies for a reason. Both mediums present romantic, idealistic fiction, and the art heist could well be Example A that the writers miss the reality mark. My art heist research found the true culprits in terrorists, mafia families, and drug dealers. The violent "deplorable trifecta" of crime. Moreover, to what aim? Mobsters and drug traffickers steal art for leverage in case law enforcement finally catches them. A plea agreement involving the return of beloved and priceless art could reduce harsh sentences.

In other words, nasty humans rob society of historic beauty just in case they are caught and need a get-out-of-jail-earlier card. The world loses a tiny piece of joy, so violent sociopaths whose sole focus is ill-gotten profit can dangle a meticulous labor of love and testament to the human spirit for decreased incarceration. A bit depressing if you really think about it.

Violent criminals compromising the legacy of geniuses. What a terrible legacy. Yet does our prioritizing the earthly criteria not yield the same consequences? You are this doing by driving the wrong direction providentially. You are compromising God's sacred plan. Or at least diluting your role, which reduces your eternal blessings.[88]

And that is the unintended consequence of living a command-number-one life. Our clamoring to live a charmed life urges us to leverage the sacred for secular pleasure and power. The eternal beauty of God's plan and creation sacrificed for instant gratification. This limits His ability to use you for maximum eternal impact.

Granted, God will realize His plan. In fact, He uses every bit of us, including the bad. The Pharisees' reign of terror via persecution caused the church to flee, which only spread the gospel to further reaches of the earth. God still uses us at our worst. Yet such acts diminish our role when we refuse to sacrifice temporal gain for eternal impact.

How do we move forward? We work to leave a legacy or trail of evidence proclaiming our contribution. Leaving a legacy drives us. Yet most people leave scant evidence by worldly standards. Chapter 10 is about fixing that, as it lays out the process of kingdom building!

---

[88] Barnicle (2021).

CHAPTER 10
DECISIONS, DECISIONS, DECISIONS

This book calls for change. While the change is internally focused, does changing your "why" require changing "where" or "what" to achieve a transformed vision? Have you considered decision-making? Which sources do you turn to when options exist and choices need to be made?

While we lean on godly wisdom, the Christian calling requires us to make tough decisions. Decision-making is a daily habit. Believers can move in several directions at the beginning, the middle (especially), and the end of our journey. Therefore, we need to spend a little ink (or pixels) examining these questions and the impact of our decisions on compounding eternal blessings.

That said, it would be wise to clear the air about a touchy subject before jumping into the topic. We each have friends who identify (or blame) God as the source of every decision. They explain away every move (especially the bad ones) with "I pray over every decision." In fact, did a romantic interest end your relationship with a nice "I just don't think God wants us to be together" send-off?

Now, certain moments call for prudence, and this is one such moment. My general theological interpretation certainly allows for seeking God in all matters. However, we must once again call upon the why question. The why is actually not "why are you asking for God's guidance in big life decisions?" but rather "why do you feel the need to tell all of us such a thing?" Also, are those answers coming from the Holy Spirit or from the pizza you had last night?

Such exclamations can be wonderful testimonies, or folks may simply be playing the "Jesus card"[2] in which no one can counter their point. Frankly, most Christians simply do not possess the adequate spiritual maturity necessary to connect for intercessory consultation. This renders most such proclamations borderline blasphemy, as folks truly are using God's name in vain.

My day job includes teaching political science at a Christian university. My academic background stressed law, urban studies, and public policy. I am not by any means a theologian. While I truly believe faith informs my lectures and structures my courses, they are government courses. Readers who purchased this book for seminary-level spiritual insight will hopefully enjoy how God has convicted one sinner regarding his thoughts and deeds toward otherness.

Teaching government is fun because most students enter the classroom doors with low expectations. Most people hate government and politics and are happy to devote as little energy and brain circuitry to the topics as possible.

Do you recall taking a government course in college or civics in high school? How about social studies or history in middle school? You probably remember facts and some concepts. A few choice morsels:
- The branches of government
- Separation of powers
- Famous founders
- The Constitution and how it got ratified
- The electoral college
- Interest groups
- Some folks took the course from a professor who stressed critical thinking. These students examined liberty, freedom, and equality

Each topic is critical to understanding democracy or government in general. We consider those concepts in my class. However, while the "what" is similar, the "how" tends to be vastly distinct. My hope is to establish a connection between topic and student. This means engaging with the material. Show it! Live it! Create an active learning experience where students exercise their minds and see the (sometimes ugly) results. Give students more than they expected and what they did not expect.

However, I am actually teaching something far more fundamental: decision-making. Indeed, the following concepts frame my class:
1. Making decisions and the emotions, criteria, and priorities driving those decisions.
2. Deciding how people will live together.
3. Seeking truth and exposing false information sources.

Let's break these categories down.

DECISION-MAKING

Who decides, and what gets decided? This remains a basic governance question. Who is in charge? The reins of power in many countries rarely pass through many hands.

Democracy is decision-making. This means big policy decisions but also individual choices (Where will I go to college? Which career or careers, getting married, and having children) as well as everyday decisions, such as where to eat lunch or whether to skip the church service. Personal decisions altering our days but also our lives. Americans not only take these decisions, both large and small, for granted but frequently loathe spending the day deciding between the convenience of fast food and the high-tone eateries.

However, making decisions is a luxury. Seriously. Few people enjoy such control over their daily comings and goings. Russian citizens do not even enjoy the luxury of setting their thermostat!5 One of the biggest decisions we make is identifying priorities. What is important to us and why? What is our belief foundation that structures how we live, where we live, and what we pursue?

Pretend life is a blank slate. Tabula rasa. No rules, no laws, no society. You can envision apocalyptic movies or simply remove every creature comfort and civilization relic you have ever known. They need answers. Most of all, they need leadership and structure.

Say someone has the bright idea to put you in charge of developing a system. How would you attack the challenge? You might start with some big questions that help identify the priorities:
- Would you err toward greater freedom or more security?
- What is the long-term decision-making process? Do you or your chosen replacement make all decisions, or a few people, or everyone?
- Who handles daily problems and arguments?
- Do you delegate and decentralize authority or keep it concentrated?
- What sort of trade market would you prefer?

These are just the "macro" policy decisions. How would you solve disputes? Where would people live? Is the population densely packed or spread out? Which economic system would society implement?

This may not sound like the government class you took, but political science considers these questions as well as the consequences of each decision. In fact, the original story for each country is critical to the way each one operates today.

Let's pretend to be Moses for a minute. The Mosaic/Sinaic covenant God made with the Hebrew nation created a template for how a group of people suddenly thrust into the wilderness would get along and survive. Indeed, Deuteronomy is often called the "preamble" of the Bible.

Frankly, modern politics owes a debt to the Sinaic covenant. Moses guided the wandering Hebrew nation toward decentralized governance. The decisions he made yielded a structure that future liberal countries could follow in distributing power. Why the Old Testament fails to receive proper recognition for such achievements is the source of another book.

So teaching government touches on deeper topics than how bills become laws. Sticking to God's plan is perhaps the hardest decision of all. Endeavoring to stay on the same path sometimes hurts even when we know it is the right direction.

So yes, my job falls under the mind-molding business. Prepare them with marketable skills. Fill their heads with information and knowledge. Teach them to think critically. However, I do a little heart molding on the side.

Think about a recent decision you have made, whether big or small. Was your choice the prudent one (the sedan with a low sticker price and high mileage per gallon, Netflix over the theater, accepting the offer from a big corporation) or perhaps riskier (that great opportunity in the Ukraine)? What drove your choice, logic, or emotions?

Most folks are loath to admit the role of emotion in their decision-making but separating our feelings from wants sounds illogical. Humans can absorb information and cultivate towering intellect, but the emotions sit at the pole position whether we are selecting investments or trying to diet yet again. Your head (and your doctor) tells you broccoli beats the hamburger, but what does the heart want?

Which emotion sits in the driver's seat? Typically fear. We worry about things we can (allegedly) control and things that escape our control. Indeed, a noted urban scholar once observed that "fear and love cannot coexist."[89] Yet fear over events shaping our lives drives our decisions, especially concerning where we live and who shares our space. Why do we allow worldly fears to undermine our understanding of the gospel and how we engage the world around us?

Combining the previous sections, where do we get intel when deciding how to live together? Which sources do we trust or mistrust? Why? Do we scrutinize information? Are we considering multiple arguments and positions, or are we resigned to binary options? Finally, do we consider new counterarguments that challenge how we see the world or are our existence and our thoughts captured inside a permanent echo chamber? What would it take to pierce this bubble?

So what drives your decisions? Do you lean on a rock-solid foundation or tilt with the breeze? Do you pursue truth and facts based on godly wisdom, or do social media algorithms provide digitalized "truth" to your inbox? Falling prey to earthly "wisdom" remains a common affliction.

SHOULD YOU STAY OR SHOULD YOU GO?

When Jesus issued command number two, the fishermen really had one choice to make. Would they keep living the life they are living or accept a challenge in uncharted waters? They decided to give up everything, including the familiar, to serve Jesus. So we will spend the remainder of this chapter asking whether it is nobler to set out for the unknown or gamely stay in place. Should you stay or should you go?

While we make several decisions during our life, staying put or leaving for unchartered waters remains the most vexing call we make. Books that examine calling typically align "the big move" with showing faith. Believers stepping out on faith with only God as their light and path. This could mean making a change to carry greater responsibility, or to take a job in an industry outside your career skill set, surrendering to ministry, moving abroad. You may even put your life at risk.

---

[89] I John 4:18 (ESV).

Other hallowed biblical figures besides Peter left something, somewhere, or someone.
- Abraham abandoned a cushy existence (by ancient standards) because God told him to father a nation.
- Nehemiah left an exalted position to renovate the Temple.
- Saul became Paul, thereby forfeiting all worldly acclaim. Leaving for bigger challenges carries drama.
- Disciples spread the Word along with the early church

Granted, Bible studies or sermons rarely extol the virtues of staying put, but God also told some important folks to stick around:
- Noah spent one hundred years building an ark and six months in the floating petting zoo.
- Everyone who left had to stay the course, especially Paul, who had all sorts of impediments, including prison and, most likely, depression.
- And we already discussed Moses, who serves as an example for both leaving and staying.

Granted, staying rarely achieves the drama and excitement of migrating to new pastures. But of course, the "why" you are making a move or staying the course matter most. Are you leaving because the job has become too difficult? Might it be someone more than something? It could be someone thanks to office politics. People have left positions for less, so this is not a critique.

That said, I have read enough calling books that focus on whether believers are happy with their work or feel fulfilled. However, lingering discomfort does not always equate to a providential nudge.

Additionally, that fulfillment void could be the Holy Spirit or something else entirely. Are you stretching yourself fully? Do you harbor doubts regarding your ability in the job? Have you fully flexed your faith muscles in this gig?

Also, have you considered the eternal impact regardless of the job title or function? God puts us where He needs us. This might be a good time as any to explore the eternal impact.

I recently finished reading Jeremiah. Good gravy. Jeremiah was a major failure by worldly standards. Everybody hated him and tried to kill him. His family wanted him dead! He led two people to the Lord. Total.

Jeremiah had no friends. Do you have a wet-blanket friend? That was Jeremiah. Everyone hated him. They threw him in prison because he was so annoying.

But Jeremiah never left his post. His calling is instructive for us. His parents thought they were raising a priest, as did Jeremiah, until God directly exclaimed that he chose Jeremiah to become a prophet when he was in his mother's womb. Jeremiah balked at the idea stressing poor speaking skills and youth.

God offered three responses to Jeremiah's objections:

Jeremiah would tell everyone what God commanded him to say. So much for youth and lack of eloquence. Follow the eternal cue cards!

God would protect Jeremiah, which turned about to be critical.

God literally touched Jeremiah's mouth to identify the message source. He said, "I have the words and just need your mouth to fulfill your calling."11

What did God touch when he appointed you? How will you be used? What human capital do you bring to the table? Jeremiah persevered through God's plan. Likewise, some of us achieved fiscal success and worldly accolades, which is awesome. Others will travel down less decorated roads. Yet everyone has a higher purpose for what they are doing, especially when God does not seem to be fulfilling His end of the bargain (or covenant) or when times are tough.

So how do you know? A small illustration from my PhD years might help. Urban economics explains (or attempts to explain) why certain cities or regions grow and why others whither. The discipline calls factors driving people to move to a certain city centrifugal forces, while centripetal forces drive people to leave. Centrifugal forces are positive macro trends such as a strong economy, employment levels, strong schools, universities, cultural amenities, or physical aesthetics. Centripetal forces include crime, pollution, or if any of the previous forces trend negative.

The Christian experience has similar forces. A good friend once made a dramatic career move because he felt similar forces, both pushing (from the current gig) and pulling (from the new gig), confirming in his mind that God was calling him to move. The Holy Spirit often works that way in our lives.

CONCLUSION: WHAT DID JIM DO?

So which move did my friend Jim make? Did his journey venture into uncharted waters, or did he stay the course? Jim's forty-year working adventure involved challenges and opportunities, much like all of our careers. Sometimes opportunity presented itself in a risky package, potentially compromising Jim's security and perhaps the ability to provide for his family in the short term. He sought God's wisdom13 and acted accordingly.

Yet the career moves or non-moves always fell under what Jim believed was God's design for his calling and career. Jim certainly enjoyed successes over the course of several decades, but he also understood the eternal purpose of his work output. The fruits of the eternal retirement account sprung forth from years of assignments and tasks that culminated in a lifetime offering to the Kingdom. And today, Jim leans on God for security while willingly delivering to the Lord's work investment returns compounded over several decades.

What does this model tell us about godly living? While we generate outcomes through our work, God really wants something different. Something *more,* in fact. This is the purpose as we explore what all these decisions mean eternally. While each of us possesses different skills and callings leveraging those skills, we learn God's ultimate outcome for our lives and legacy is the same.

CHAPTER 11
THE MIDDLE

> "In this you rejoice, though now for a little while, if necessary, you have been grieved by various trials, so that the tested genuineness of your faith—more precious than gold that perishes though it is tested by fire—may be found to result in praise and glory and honor at the revelation of Jesus Christ. Though you have not seen him, you love him. Though you do not now see him, you believe in him and rejoice with joy that is inexpressible and filled with glory, obtaining the outcome of your faith, the salvation of your souls."
> —1 Peter 1: 6-9 ESV

Our journey together has reached the shore, as sailors say. The end is near. You may have mixed feelings at the moment. Either way, it will all be over soon, whether that brings pain or rejoicing.

We always focus on the beginning and the end. Right? This is how we consume culture. Authors and movie producers alike realize the story must catch our attention quickly. Some of my favorite movie scenes opened the story. Action movies with bullets flying, science fiction with spaceships hurling past stars, romcoms I put on ignore.

And who can forget your favorite author describing a key character from physique to cranial capacity? Or books that took a page from screenplays by throwing you in the middle of action or drama?

Of course, creations like this book are (hopefully) leading somewhere. You invested time and money, after all. Great art fully immerses the audience in the narrative, so everyone wants to know the fate of favorite characters, the world, what have you. Everything builds to a dramatic conclusion.

The beginning grabs our attention, and the ending sticks with us. Christians specifically focus on the salvation experience and the rearview mirror phase of the walk, where we reminisce on accomplishments and outcomes. We read biographies of great leaders or creators focused on the triumphs and the end of the trail. Everyone prefers completion, as it allows us to take stock of what someone accomplished. We like to keep score on human activity.

Speaking of keeping score, have you ever seriously considered what the resume of any saint or biblical figure might look like? I led a Bible study on Romans once where my first visual was comparing Saul's resume with Paul's CV. Saul achieved a learned and elite status with sterling recommendations which Paul relinquished. That is Kingdom building!

What about Peter's resume? Peter's jobs or positions-held section would include being a disciple of Christ with strong evidence he was the chief spokesperson of the group. Peter certainly enjoyed a prominent role among the twelve based on scriptural evidence.[90] He clearly assumed leadership of the church and extended community after the crucifixion, including speaking at Pentecost and driving the appointment of St. Matthias as the replacement for Judas. He served as judge, jury, and advocate for the faith and those entering the faith, including paving the path for Gentiles to enter by the Spirit as opposed to the Law. Indeed, Paul's first post-conversion wish was meeting with Peter.

Yet the two letters Peter the Apostle wrote at the end of his life and mission illustrate a different impact of the Christian walk. Peter could have easily focused on outcomes. His list was extensive. But this passage is not accomplishment-driven. Peter describes how the journey affected him. How a life spent pursuing God's plan while rejecting comfort and security forges our faith.

Peter could spend a lifetime spinning yarns about the process. In fact, he did. I recall listening to a well-known retired pastor delivering a guest sermon one Sunday. Are you familiar with the humble brag? Dr. Pastor of a megachurch turned convention president sure did. The

---

[90] Granted, he was clearly the loudest disciple who often spoke without thinking, so this certainly contributed to his prominence.

church I built and then tripled enrollment? Means nothing in the eyes of God. My honorary doctorate from ye old alma mater? Dirt in the eyes of God. He spent a good hour reciting the resume line by line that meant nothing to God. A friend leaned over, asking, "Does the guy need a gig?"

I am well-versed in both the humble and not so humble bragging incarnations. I am from Texas, after all. Bragging is a human (especially male) pastime. Weaving a story laced with your greatness is a wonderfully subversive form of cheap PR. Few people are completely above a little humble brag.

Peter is not bragging humbly or otherwise. He is not even throwing out the "great ways God used me" line of speech. An accurate title for 1 and 2 Peter would be "This Is What God Did to Me" as opposed to "This Is What God Did Through Me."

God challenged Peter and his faith. The apostle experienced trials at unimaginable levels. He sacrificed the life he knew for the unknown with prison or persecution as a reward. But Peter experienced a transformation. His courage and uncompromising leadership landed him in prison and ultimately rewarded him with a violent, painful death. His was hardly the path of least resistance, as God transformed Peter's stubborn nature into innovative leadership that directed the church across fields unknown.

The cocky, smack-talking, Jesus-denying fool morphed into a wise, courageous leader who left it all on the table.

It's hard to leave it all on the table without God changing you. The world blurs our vision with a desire for short-term gratification. Godly wisdom realizes that we cannot see all the fruits of our toil, at least in our earthly form.

We talked about generations in chapter 5 and how the boomers rejected their parents' life. Well, my sons did not so much reject my life structure and philosophy, but they did reject my high school extracurricular activities by choosing theater over football and sports.

Good choice.

My oldest son even took up musical theater during his senior year. Granted, he did more dancing than singing. Still, very impressive coming from a family with little rhythm or pitch.

The show was *Big Fish,* and it had an interesting twist. The main character, Ed Bloom, is a dreamer who constantly annoys his son Will with tall tales from his life. Their relationship (or lack thereof) structures the narrative.

Ed's first story regales Will of his father visiting a witch when he was in high school. The witch tells Ed and his friends how they will die. He handles the news with an eerie calm.

Would you want to know? Science fiction dabbles constantly in eternity and mortality. Mere mortals can learn how they die, when they die, or where they die. Time travel writers often transport people to their very own gravesite. Some stories dealt with characters who knew facts regarding their demise, while others portrayed characters seeking an eternal exit strategy. Several scripts personified death. These always interested me the most, especially during the formative years. The actor always played death as a calm, soothing counselor whose job mandated simply guiding the dying character gently to his or her fate. And the rub was always death was better than their current existence. What they sought to possess and keep (life) was actually worse than the fate they fought so desperately to avoid (death).

This was Ed Bloom's response to learning the how of his earthly demise. Ed not only accepted his fate but appreciated the freedom that the knowledge carried with it. It was freedom from fear. Ed met every precarious moment life threw at him with a shrug. He knew how his story ended.[91]

We Christians know how our stories end, but do we live like it?

WHY

Peter knew how he was going to die very early in his ministry. Remember John 16? The classic "feed my sheep" passage? We already touched on that Peter-Jesus exchange during the shame chapter. However, we need to isolate verse 18:

---

[91] August, John. "Big Fish." Based on the novel by John Wallace and the Columbia Motion Picture written by John August.

> Very truly I tell you, when you were younger you dressed yourself and went where you wanted; but when you are old you will stretch out your hands, and someone else will dress you and lead you where you do not want to go." Jesus said this to indicate the kind of death by which Peter would glorify God. Then he said to him, "Follow me!"[92]

Peter learned that his would not be a peaceful ending. It would be loud, painful, and perhaps worst of all, he would be at the mercy of his enemies. So much to sacrifice.

However, Peter pulled an Ed. Read the verse at the beginning of this chapter again. Trials that test our faith but ultimately refine it. Peter clearly says you must experience the pain to grow. It is non-negotiable.

Peter's life hammers home God's desired outcome. He clearly cares about our actions, our sin of both commission and omission, and even our tiniest impact on eternity. God cares about those things. Like Paul's missionary journeys or even Jim's retirement funds.

However, God is less concerned about what we do or achieve and more focused on who we become. How the sacrifice and comfort-averse risk-seeking molds us, cracks the mold into slithers of clay and builds us back again one providential step at a time. The process is painful yet essential.

And how do you become the person God desires absent the challenges we have covered? He seeks disciples who embrace sacrifice and resist the comfort zone. Those who are aware of their fears but face them nonetheless.

This is why Jim funded his ERA in the first place. It's a bit of a paradox, really. God needs us to carry out His plan and blesses us with gifts and abilities, but we must rely on Him to maximize our calling.

Let's review Jim's testimony one final time for the instructive impact. He toiled for more than four decades in a career. He sacrificed his time in carrying out his calling as employee and provider.

---

[92] John 21: 18 (ESV).

Jim's sacrifice only starts with working nine to five. He was prudent, saved early and often, thus triggering compounding returns. He could have devoted all discretionary income to creature comforts or exotic trips. And maybe his family enjoyed such luxuries from time to time. However, Jim and his wife intentionally planned for their post-working years by setting aside income. This was a smart move to ensure future comfort and security.

And now they are in the process of giving it all away to God! Jim and his wife continue to forego creature comforts in the name of eternal blessings. While this is an incredible outcome, it only happened because God shaped them through their walk. It remains more about who they became than what they did. Focus on the latter and you can be big in the eyes of the world, but you must focus on the former to yield compounding eternal blessings.

And that is how your walk can yield compounding blessings. This book did not outline a blueprint for worldly success or financial independence. Frankly, the narrative renders action subservient to a mindset. Why? I once had a Christian counselor/psychologist explain that he believed the brain drives our actions. So he treated clients accordingly. The cheating husband? Draw his focus away from the partner and all circumstances surrounding the affair. Compulsive eaters? Do not focus on circumstances, events, or emotions compelling stressful eating.

What's The Plan? Followed this model in a sense. We identified why living sacrificially devoid of comfort and security brings us closer to and more reliant on God. And while this is not a book about outcomes, that is God's ultimate desired outcome. This is a lifelong process, as the book fleshed out. We learned that God needs us. This means every action or decision we make impacts eternity. This is true whether our days are spent on the African mission field tending the village crops or in a courtroom defending a client. Providence/The Holy Spirit utilizes our outcomes for Kingdom significance.

Given this revelation, we spent the rest of our time together discovering how to maximize our time on this rock. Stories have beginnings, middle transitions, and endings. Our life script is no different, and our journey together followed this model. The words on each page encouraged readers to lay an eternal foundation early in their calling. We met Jim and his ERA. One of the best pieces of advice I received was to identify people whose career/calling aligned with your career vision and follow in their pattern. Jim provided readers their Kingdom pattern. Bottom line, you need a God-ordained plan, and Jim provided that model.

Inevitably, your plan incurs barriers. Sadly, we are frequently the biggest barriers to fulfilling God's calling. The hardest decisions are made in "the middle," or what I refer to as the montage-calling phase. We seek a better understanding of God's plans and whether it mandates staying the course or plotting a new path.

Yet the world plants barrier seeds early in our lives, often without our fully acknowledging or understanding the damage created. Chapter 7 identified and examined the "taunts that haunt" a lifetime if we let them. The circumstances change by generation, but the impact is often the same. This chapter provided a critical analysis of long-term emotional scar tissue that requires healing.

The final chapters provided a rear-view mirror perspective. How we see what our lives accomplished, but most importantly, why we ended up on our chosen path. Chapter 9 also argued that, yes, living the Christian walk is scary, but the consequences of failing to do so are scarier, broader in scope, and permanent. Better to follow God's treacherous (to our eyes) path than the well-worn earthly trail.

My prayer is that my written musings help us yield endless blessings that eclipse our time here!

What does eternal impact look like? How can we touch the heavens? Our creations/work can outlive us. Movies remain relevant long after actors and directors have left us. We sing songs written and performed by late artists. Great art surpasses time, as do great books.[93] Yet most people come and go leaving little evidence of their existence.

We will most likely never know in this life how God used us.

Can I use one more political/historical example? John Tyler was the tenth United States President. Tyler packed many accolades into his seventy-two years. He was both governor of his home state of Virginia and represented the state in the United States Senate prior to turning forty. Tyler engaged in numerous high-profile policy affairs,

---

[93] One can only hope.

including, most notably, the annexation of my home state of Texas. Yet Tyler hardly registers historically, and that is not merely due to the passage of time as some of his contemporaries still garner historical ink and analysis. Indeed, my interest in Tyler stems completely from my youngest son recently declaring Tyler's successor, James K. Polk, as his favorite American president.[94]

Yet Tyler's legacy remains fresh for other reasons totally unrelated to his political career. In fact, his parenting skills possibly outlived his public career. Tyler had fifteen children with two wives over the course of forty-five years! He became a widower and married a second time to a woman thirty years his junior while serving in the White House from 1841–1845.

Tyler and Julia, his second wife, have seven children together. Julia gave birth to Lyon in 1853. Lyon rose to prominence in his own right as a historian and eventually president of his (and his father's) alma mater, The College of William & Mary.[95] So Lyon achieved success in his chosen field, much like his father.

He shared other traits with dear old dad. His first wife died in 1921, and Lyon subsequently married a much younger woman (a thirty-five-year gap) that same year. They had three children in addition to three from his first marriage. While one died in infancy, the two other sons are still living well into their nineties as of this writing.

In summary, John Tyler's familial legacy includes two grandsons still living 230 years after his birth in 1790! Now that is some legacy!

What lessons can we take from this, and how do John Tyler's career and extensive family tree speak to calling? A few morsels.

1. Our legacy continues whether the world notices or acknowledges it. People rarely think "John Tyler" when living in or talking about Texas, but it's part of his destiny.
2. At some point, we will have no choice but to surrender control to God and hand over the reins of power. The

---

[94] Cole was twelve when he first proudly announced this decision like he had won the lottery. One of his best friends is a big Andrew Jackson fan, and they argue constantly over who was the better president. And yes, not one girl in sight!

[95] Lyon's grandfather actually roomed with Thomas Jefferson, so the family's roots run deep with the college.

sooner this happens, the better.
3. We never truly know how God uses our time here or what He will use.
4. Building on number 3, we focus so much on our work product as the legacy building blocks, but other things (see family) matter.

The world is fickle. What passes for fame and legacy sometimes offers little in the way of substance. It is all so fleeting, but God is eternal and can use us for eternity if we only let Him.

CHAPTER 12
THE ORIGINAL TITLE OF THIS BOOK AND ITS MEANING

Let's talk about first jobs. I delivered drinks at football games, bagged groceries, waited tables. I have had grunt jobs, if you will. Those gigs are good for you. They give you perspective. Even that first big person/post-collegiate gig can be humbling. Part of life, right?

My first gig out of school was a breathtaking foray into the world of mortgage banking. Most folks deal with mortgage banks (what we called our employer) or mortgage company/servicer (what customer called us) at some point, thanks to their status as homeowners. You send payments to the company, resolve issues, refinance, and pay property taxes indirectly.

My role was in default. Not fun. Managing irate customers who could not make payments. I left that role with several sacred lessons in tow. Here is one that hopefully encourages you today.

My boss was an innovative thinker who held that specific position because his boss was an innovative thinker. This being the private sector, they were always looking for ways to save money, which thankfully did not include jettisoning me! In fact, they tasked me and a coworker with researching ways to increase the number of loans each representative managed. Efficiency is the fancy term for this, although this article is not about efficiency.

Well, our little tag team pressed forward with clear marching orders. The first report submitted for approval from our bosses was an analysis of everything default processors did daily. After all, how can you figure out how to increase what a person does unless you know what he or she does? The report identified each task, how long it normally took, and how many times processors engaged in that every day.

We delivered the fancy report to the bosses. The big boss took thirty seconds to review it and asked how we determined our numbers. How? It was simple. We found the weekly statistics and divided them by forty to calculate daily averages. People work eight hours per day for five days every week. Genius right? We had our annual bonus speeches written in advance.

We never made those speeches. Instead, we spent what seemed like forty hours explaining our methodology. The big boss summarized our failure thusly: "People never work an eight-hour day. Yes, they may be in the office from eight to five with lunch, but they are not spending eight hours at their desk producing work. They meander around the office talking to people, chat at the water cooler, read, handle personal stuff. They probably at best work eighty-five percent of scheduled work time per day."

Then he launched the verbal haymaker. "Your data omits a margin of error. Add it, and then we can talk."

Okay, this was amazing. First, our bosses realized we were wasting time. I mean, we all did at times, but man, I had nightmares where they found me wandering around chatting up the accounting team. Nevertheless, they clearly knew about this part of the work culture. In addition, I am dating myself by noting this conversation occurred prior to the Internet age but only ever so slightly. The eighty-five-percent estimate seems optimistic these days thanks to social media, podcasting, the Internet, and so on.

However, the margin of error concept stuck with me. Did I give my coworkers or employees a margin of error? What about my bosses? Does the concept extend to personal matters? Did I give my family a margin of error? If so, did they return the favor? What about my family now? Do I give my wife a margin of error? What about my sons?

Does this concept extend to spiritual matters? Do I give God a margin of error? That sounds heretical. Why does the perfect Creator need a margin of error? Perhaps the more theologically safe question is, "Do I expect God's calling for my life to need a margin of error?" In other words, "Does my perception of God's vision for my life need a little restructuring?" Maybe my timing and progress-measuring benchmarks fall out of alignment when it comes to the eternal.

How does this process operate (or fail to operate) in my finite brain? Well, I expect certain events or results to happen at certain appointed times without delay. Moreover, without barriers from other people or cataclysmic events forcing me in a different direction.

What about you? Do you give God a margin of error? I ask about the MOE specifically because I needed that margin before penning the first sentence of this book. *What's The Plan?* Was not the original title for this book. I will explain shortly why it changed. My first working title was *The Eternal Retirement Account or ERA,* which was a problem quickly brought to my attention by agent and editor alike. And the title certainly had issues. The book market includes several works covering what seems like pretty much every possible angle of retirement. This includes books on retirement preparation, saving for retirement, spending in retirement, living in retirement, how long you might be retired, working in retirement. You get the idea.

However, the bigger problem is this book, as you can hopefully ascertain, is not about retirement at all. In fact, it is not written specifically for generations approaching retirement, but rather anyone grappling with the concept of God's calling at any phase of life. That topic actually speaks to younger generations more than seasoned professionals, but it has timeless qualities.

So yes, ERA was a bad title. Kudos to my agent and editor. However, the spirit of that title, if you will, still permeates this work and connects the criteria. It also is deeply woven into my purpose for writing the book. I want to dive into that, but a word on retirement as a concept if you will indulge me.

I fully understand any potential confusion. This book is a call to action, and retirement is seen as the exact opposite. The ending, as opposed to the genesis or even the middle, of your calling story. I take issue with that retirement vision, but that does accurately portray most Americans' image of retirement as a destination. And make no mistake, this destination occupies the mindset of many folks.

Interestingly, retirement is a fairly recent historical development but not an American-made construct. Retirement actually originated in Germany. Indeed, the famed Chancellor Otto Von Bismarck developed the German retirement system, which offered state support to "those who are disabled from work by age and invalidity [and] have a well-grounded claim to care from the state" in an ongoing effort to address youth unemployment.[96] It is an odd twist that retirement programs exist

---

[96] Pasricha, *Why Retirement Is a Flawed Concept.* Harvard Business Review, April 2016.

to enhance opportunities for younger workers by removing seasoned professionals from the job market. The American Social Security system pursued this goal. Bismarck also feared socialist incursions, so he also viewed the policy as a pillar for economic efficiency. Regardless of the policy goal, Germany provided social insurance starting in 1889 for workers seventy and over by matching mandatory worker contributions. This might sound familiar as it was the model for the American Social Security program, which launched some seventy years later.[97]

These early public programs provided for workers whose most productive years were behind them and who needed an escape hatch from a rapidly developing economy that no longer valued whatever skills they possessed. The payout term was expected to be short, given that workers received nothing prior to their seventieth birthday, which was the life expectancy in Germany during the industrial revolution age. It was a modest commitment structured to remove workers past their prime from the workforce and hopefully provide an opportunity to live out their final years outside of squalor.[98]

My, how things have changed. Bismarck and the Social Security architects would not grasp the cottage industry that retirement has wrought. Retirement is not merely a destination, as mentioned earlier, but a goal. Workers at all levels feed off advertising and "analysis," encouraging them to plan for retirement almost daily. Yes, this includes important financial considerations, but that is merely the beginning. Blogs, podcasts, and books exist to help you plan how you will retire, when you will retire, and where you will retire.

And the destination is no longer limited to the "golden years" of sixty-five-plus or whatever is considered old these days. I know (hope) you, my dear readers, are not all within the traditional retirement-age window. However, what is that window now? Retirement and planning for it is a huge industry that gets its fair share of coverage. Indeed, the FIRE movement (Financial Independence, Retire Early) has changed the retirement purpose. Folks young and old envision retirement and the capital necessary for that stage as a transitional opportunity to live life and define work on your own terms. You

---

[97] Otto Von Bismarck. Social Security History. SSA.gov.
[98] Ibid.

sacrifice time in exchange for compensation or entrepreneurial equity to fulfill a passion or purpose. Your work product has meaning beyond sustaining your lifestyle. Again, the FIRE movement has produced endless sources of material explaining how to leave your boss behind prior to your thirtieth birthday and what to do with your remaining decades on the planet.[99]

While experts could envision a FIRE-type movement, the Great Resignation has sprung up out of nowhere thanks to the Covid pandemic. Yet its origins and philosophy are similar to the FIRE movement while also involving the younger generations of workers. Buoyed by a combo platter of unemployment payments, debt deferrals, and frankly an unprecedented number of entrepreneurial opportunities flowing from the digital landscape, younger workers are quitting what many consider dead-end jobs or, at best, entry-level positions to strike out on their own and tote their own note, as it were. The younger generations clearly believe the digital economy offers greater rewards to those building their own stake. Who can blame them?[100]

This begs the question: What does everyone want from retirement or these alternatives that the daily grind does not provide? Well, we call it the daily grind for a reason. Waking up early to get ready to trudge your way to the office or cubicle. It wears on people.

I have a theory about the daily grind. Of course, I do. There is ample evidence in support of said theory. The daily grind, and working in general, remain cumbersome because we have no choice but to keep at it thanks to debt, lifestyles costs, and other costs of living. Indeed, Americans listed flexibility as one of three main things they wanted from retirement.[101] The other two were financial security and time with family.

---

[99] Kerr, 2011.Kerr, Alexandra. *Financial Independence, Retire Early (FIRE)*. Investopedia.com. November 22, 2021. *https://www.investopedia.com/terms/f/financial-independence-retireeearly-fire.asp*

[100] Thompson, Derek, *The Great Resignation Is Accelerating*. The Atlantic. October 15, 2021. *https://www.theatlantic.com/ideas/archive/2021/10/great-resignation-accelerating/620382/*

[101] Hopkins Jamie, *3 Things Most Americans Want in Retirement and How to Get Them*, Forbes.com. May 26, 2017. *https://www.forbes.com/sites/jamiehopkins/2017/05/26/3-things-most-americans-want-in-retirement-and-how-to-get-them/?sh=7b7cb26834bc*

Flexibility yields power. Flexibility means we choose what we want to do when we want to do it. It facilitated other activities such as travel, volunteering, golf, and time with grandchildren or grandparents if you are part of the FIRE generation. Flexibility offers control.

And that is how the concept of retirement birthed this book. I considered the American retirement model and its inconsistency with God's plan. The retirement dream essentially revolves around (in my mind, at least) our finally calling all the shots in our life untethered by corporate structure and the commute. Moreover, the shots we call usually result in greater comfort, instant gratification, and other perceived benefits. All the worldly criteria we are battling.

I get it. Believe me, these are the battles I have all the time. Retirement dreams are not sins in their own right; they just lead us down the wrong path potentially.

However, alternatives do exist. Jim's testimony taught us that. Honestly, his sacrifice heavily influenced this book. Long-term planning typically means thirty to forty years, but Jim thinks bigger. And longer. His ERA funded God-sized plans.

Elly also taught us a different way. Follow God's plan even when it takes down an unknown path. You must also fully commit to His plan as opposed to looking for the exit.

Is that the type of flexibility you want from retirement? Can we Americans, yearning to unplug, realize the eternal opportunities before us and act accordingly? Bottom line, do you yearn to bring eternal value to God's Kingdom daily regardless of the life phase?

It is probably safe to call me a data junky. Granted, I wrote a quantitatively driven dissertation. Still, it would be hard to refer to myself as an expert. Yet that experience does give me a sense of both the value and limitation of pretty numbers.

While I use data, I am definitely a sports fan. Team executives and fans alike historically used statistics to distinguish the best players from, well, everyone else. Data analysis has turned this method on its head and changed how we identify productive players from those needing to trade the bat or helmet for an insurance license or teaching certificate.

One of my favorites is the +/- because the value lies in the simplicity. It tracks individual player performance but definitely helps coaches determine which players should play together and when to play certain team members during what part of the game. Basically, you calculate the score when a player was in the game. Hockey created the tool, but several NBA teams measure +/- so we will use a basketball illustration since it is a more popular sport and a richer example. Say your favorite hoops squad dropped a weeknight game one hundred to ninety-five, but the +/- for a seldom-used guard was forty to twenty-three. This means your team outscored the evil opposition by seventeen points when this ball handler graced the court. Maybe your favorite team needs a new coach.

The +/- offers numerous ways to help teams best utilize personnel. That said, this is not an NBA analytics article. This is a spiritual- and eternal-calling piece. What is your calling +/-? Also, how can we measure it and improve it?

The +/- measures value. How much value does a player bring on the court? Likewise, we should ask how God could use us to bring value to His Kingdom. How can we be Kingdom influencers or more effective Kingdom influencers?

In addition, how do we measure eternal value and then develop a value improvement plan? First, what about developing a list of value-driven activities:

- Time in the Word
- Quiet time
- Prayer
- Bible studies
- Finding godly mentors

This is a good but hardly all-encompassing list. Still, we grow by spending time with God and other positive believers. Bottom line, these activities should enhance our value.

However, data analytics is a limited tool, as I previously mentioned. What is the biggest limitation? Well, people analyze data, and our cranial capacity remains finite regardless of degrees and accolades.

Yet the biggest data analysis limitation is the chosen criteria. While quantitative information provides perhaps the best form of measurement, pretty numbers are pretty worthless unless we know that we are measuring or what we are measuring for in many cases. People fail to understand that we cannot measure value without defining value. Moreover, our value definition is worldly, temporal, and ultimately worthless in God's scheme.

So measuring your value and seeking to enhance your value begins and ends with seeking God's definition of value. He measures our value using an eternal metric or rubric. Therefore, we should contrast worldly criteria with the eternal standards and focus on the latter list. This is not meant to be a works standard but recalibrating our hearts and minds to determine what is truly sacred.

Peter never possessed the luxury of retirement during his days, but he openly rejected everything modern Americans crave in retirement. Peter never sought control over his affairs or future. Comfort was the last thing on his mind. While Peter experienced much success and saw the fruits of his labor during his lifetime, his true legacy only emerged post-mortem. Speaking of death, Jesus promised Peter's would be painful and at the hands of his enemies. Peter accepted that fate and eternity is better for it.

Retirement is a blessed landmark. None of us should feel guilt over preparing financially and emotionally to detach from daily burdens. Yet Jim and his wife model the potential for what that phase can become: a time where we commit to the timeless. Of course, why wait? We can accelerate our commitment starting right now!

ROBERT JOSEPH SULLIVAN

Dr. Sullivan is an emerging thought leader in politics and policy, urban studies, and the Christian walk. His role weaves through several areas from the classroom to the boardroom, but everything flows from serving students. He currently serves as Dean of the College of Humanities & Social Sciences, but the classroom perhaps remains his first love. Rob believes that connecting with students remains the most critical classroom skill. He believes material should engage and entertain and learning expands beyond dumping information on fertile brains. Rob's writing is no different.

Rob has served at Dallas Baptist University for over twenty years. He assumed a strategic role soon after joining the institution. While all of this sounds so official or, perhaps, academic, Rob's real purpose is to help others realize why God put us here and how we can thrive. This passion served as a God-driven signal forging a commitment to education access, empowerment, and public policy addressing these initiatives.

Rob's academic background and research interests also stress law, urban studies, and public policy. He earned a BS at Howard Payne University, JD at the University of Texas at Austin, and a PhD at the University of Texas at Arlington. He recently authored Valuable Partnerships, an examination of Texas municipalities leveraging innovation, and an American government textbook.

Like all good Texas boys, Rob grew up on the gridiron, ultimately accepting a scholarship from Howard Payne University after serving as a team captain in his high school team. A tumultuous freshman year included a traumatic knee injury, effectively ending the football phase of life. Yet this served as an early lesson that God closes doors for a reason as Rob accepted Jesus in the spring of that year. This clearly altered Rob's path and leadership priorities. "God kept putting leadership roles in front of me, so I just followed." Indeed, those roles included SGA president and Student Foundation president.

After graduating from HPU with honors, Rob pursued a J.D. from the University of Texas. He initially worked in the mortgage industry, steadily accepting more significant responsibility in default management until sensing God's call to higher education. That said, he believes God uses every vocation or avocation for the Kingdom. "Providence moves in ways beyond our comprehension. Our job is to serve."

Rob has invested nearly two decades in what he considers the Kingdom building business. Working with college students of various ages and life stages stressed to Rob the many factors driving Believers to and from God's plan for their life. He fully ascribes to this holistic approach to mentoring and developing Kingdom builders that extend beyond skill honing and networking to nothing less than mind and heart refinement. "This process incorporates all aspects of one's existence."

God communicated this vision to Rob via vocation but also family. Lea and Rob married in 1998 after meeting in Sunday school. Lea has profound hearing loss since birth. Rob is continuously amazed by Lea's talent and resilience but was surprised by the emotional toll living in a hearing world exacts on his bride. "Coming from a broken home and the emotional aftermath accompanying that, I understand how certain things stick with us regardless of where the journey leads." Rob and Lea have two sons. Alec and Cole, as well as Caesar the Australian Shepherd.

Rob finds it nearly impossible to identify a favorite book in the bible or verse. Jeremiah sticks out because it is fifty-two chapters of resilience. In addition, he focuses on outcomes, so Micah 6:8 is important:

> He has shown you, O mortal, what is good.
> And what does the LORD require of you?
> To act justly and to love mercy
> and to walk humbly with your God.

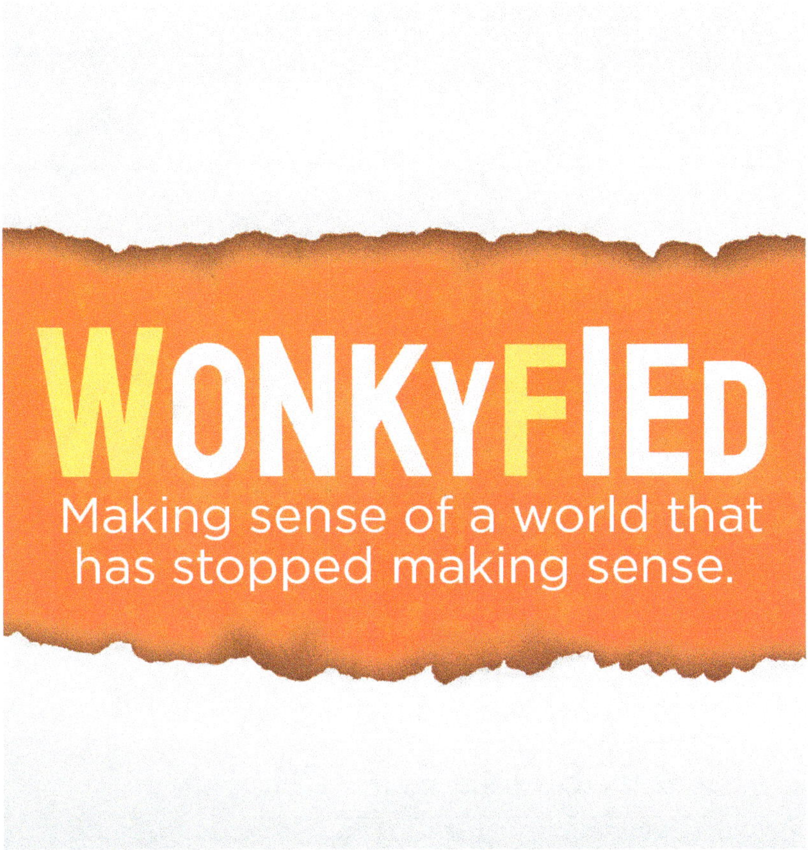

WONKYFIED
Making sense of a world that has stopped making sense.

You can listen to more great stories and interviews at
http://drrobsullivan.com/podcast/
or anywhere you listen to podcasts, you will find
Wonkyfied with Dr. Robert Sullivan

PURPOSE. PEOPLE.

POSSESSIONS PRAYER.

PROFESSIONS. POLITICS.

PLACE. PRAISE.

Check out our website at: *www.drrobsullivan.com*
Engage in our Pretty Good Blog and listen to our podcast to help you
Make sense of a world that has stopped making sense!
Connect with us and let us know what things you struggle with making sense of in this world! We would love to hear from you.
robert@drrobertsullivan.com

www.ingramcontent.com/pod-product-compliance
Lightning Source LLC
Chambersburg PA
CBHW050324120526
44592CB00014B/2043